Wood Pellet Smoker and Grill Cookbook

3 Books in 1: Wood Pellet Smoker and Grill Cookbook, Wood Pellet Recipe Book and Blank Recipe Book

Adam Greenwood

Table of Contents
Book 1

Book 2

Book 3

BOOK 1

Wood Pellet Smoker and Grill Cookbook

The Complete Guide for Your Barbecue. Lots of Tasty and Delicious Recipes (Also for Rubs, Marinades, Sauces), Teaching You the Best Techniques to Grill Everything, From Meat and Fish to Vegetable Plus Tips and Tricks for Beginners and Advanced

Adam Greenwood

Introduction

Are you bored and tired of spending hours together in front of your regular conventional grill only to have the food unevenly cooked? Does your grilled food taste more like coal than the meat flavor? Are you looking for an easier way to get the desired delicious and smoky flavor into your meats and other foods? If yes, then it is time to upgrade your conventional grill and try out the wood pellet smoker and grill.

This book is perfect for new wood pellet grill owners or those who want to trade their old grilling methods for a new one. In the course of this book, you will learn about the structure and components of a wood pellet smoker grill, the reasons why cooking with it is amazing, and a few simple tips on how to use it. You will also learn about flavorful food-grade wood pellets to perfectly complement everyday ingredients to obtain incredible results. By using the various cooking tips and tricks discussed in this book, you can grill meats like a professional chef.

This book has loads of wood pellet smoker grill recipes using different meats as well as veggies. All these recipes are incredibly easy to follow, are divided into different categories for your convenience—and they include recipes for delicious rubs, marinades sauces, and glazes. These simple and delicious recipes yield incredible results.

Now you can impress your friends and family with a perfectly cooked and smoked piece of meat at the next barbecue party. The best part is you could do all this without any of the hassles usually associated with grilling and smoking. All you have to do is make sure that your pantry is stocked with the required ingredients, choose a recipe that you fancy, make some kick-ass glaze, sauce or marinade and get started! Soon you will be the BBQ expert, as your friends and family members seek invites to your coveted grills and BBQ nights.

If you are ready to learn more about this and get started, read on. Thank you for choosing this book, I hope you enjoy it.

Chapter 1:

What is a Wood Pellet Smoker Grill

Pellet grills are versatile outdoor cookers that efficiently combine the elements of different cooking appliances, such as smoker, oven, and gas or charcoal grills. As the name suggests, pellet grills use wood pellets as the fuel source. Ingredients can be cooked via direct or indirect heat, depending on the placement of the rack Understanding the inner workings, structure, and components of the wood pellet smoker grill helps make the most of its features. Even if it seems a little overwhelming initially, it is quite straightforward.

Structure of a Wood Pellet Smoker Grill

A wood pellet smoker grill consists of a hopper, firepot, auger, hot rod, heat deflector, induction fan, resistance temperature detector, flame zone pan, and grease bucket.

The part of the appliance where the wood pellets are filled is known as the hopper. The firepot is the area directly under the grill where the fire is lit. The auger helps to transport the wood pellets from the hopper to the firepot. The hot rod or the igniter element ignites the flame to start a fire once the wood pellets are in the firepot.

The induction fan present in this appliance helps to stoke the flames and evenly distribute the heat. These elements turn the regular grill and smoker into an appliance with functionalities similar to an oven. The temperature of the grill and smoker is measured by the resistance temperature detector.

There exists a barrier between the flames in the firepot and the grill known as the heat deflector. It helps redirect the heat to promote even cooking while reducing the risk of burning or charring. You can use the flame zone pan coupled with griddle accessories and a searing grate to grill foods at high temperatures without using a barrier to separate the two. Using a grease bucket prevents any fats or oils from dripping into the flames.

Why Choose This?

Wood pellet smoker grills are user-friendly so, irrespective whether you are a newbie or a pro, grilling and smoking meats is easy. You don't have to worry about any sudden flare-ups so ensuring an even cook on the meats is almost always guaranteed. It also reduces the risk of charring meat due to exposure to uneven temperatures.

This is an incredible appliance with multiple uses. You can grill and smoke a variety of meats, seafood, and poultry. You can also use it instead of an oven. You can cook sides, appetizers, and even desserts on a wood pellet grill. By merely changing the placement of the ingredients between the top and lower racks and varying the temperature, you can use it to cook a variety of ingredients.

In the previous section, you were introduced to the basic structure and components of a typical wood pellet smoker grill. That's about it. There is no learning curve involved here. When in doubt, follow the instructions given in the recipes shared in the subsequent chapters of this book, and cook like a pro!

Wood pellet smoker grills are cost- and fuel-efficient. They need around a pound of wood pellets per hour of cooking time. Another benefit of this incredible appliance is that you don't have to worry about transferring or lugging any heavy propane tanks. So, they are safer and easier to use.

If you love the idea of grilled and smoked foods, but don't have the time or patience for it, this is the perfect appliance for you. For instance, to get the best results, you need to smoke meat overnight. Rub the meat with a dry rub or a marinade, set the temperature on the wood pellet smoker grill, and leave it overnight! Yes, it is as simple as that!

Another advantage of the wood pellet smoker grill is that the external temperature does not affect the cooking procedure. As long as the internal temperature of the grill is maintained, you have nothing to worry about.

How to Use a Wood Pellet Smoker Grill

Before you start using the wood pellet smoker grill, ensure that you give it a dry run. It helps to burn any traces of contaminants, chemicals, and other pollutants that might have been leftover from the manufacturing process. The burn-in procedure is quite simple. Simply fill the hopper and half the firepot with wood pallets and plug in the appliance. Set the temperature between 350–450°F and the flames will last for an hour. Don't forget to go through the instruction manual to check the ideal temperature for the dry run.

To improve the overall results obtained from the wood pellet grill, season the grill before you start cooking. The simplest way to season the grill is by cooking bacon at 350°F for about an hour.

If you want your food to be infused only with clean smoke whenever you cook, ensure that you clean this appliance. It hardly takes a couple of minutes to clean the smoker grill. Clean the grill grates using a wire brush while they're still hot and then wipe them with a warm cloth or paper towel. When the fire pot is completely cool, remove the drip pan and use a degreaser to clean it thoroughly. Always remove all traces of ash from the body of the grill and the firepot. If the ash starts piling up, the overall efficiency of the grill reduces. Ensure that there are no traces of old grease after you use the wood pellet smoker grill.

About Food-Grade Wood Pellets

Whenever you purchase wood pellets for the smoker grill, ensure that you use food-grade barbecue wood pellets. These specific pellets do not contain any harmful chemicals and foreign pollutants. They also don't have any additives except for vegetable oils which reduce the ash that's left over after grilling and smoking. Food-grade wood chips are usually cylindrical with a 1/4-inch diameter.

Food-grade wood pellets usually come in a combination of flavors that are either made from oak or alder. Each type of wood has a specific flavor that pairs well with certain types of meats. The percentage of the flavor varies from one manufacturer to another.

To improve the overall taste and smoke intensity of the resultant product, pair wood pallets with specific foods. For instance, apple has a strong aroma that smells and pairs incredibly well with all types of game meats, pork, poultry, and lamb. Alder pairs well with fatty fish such as salmon, pork poultry, beef, and lamb because of its mild and sweet taste and aroma. Cherry wood has a slightly sweet flavor that lends a rosy hue to the meats. Cherry wood chips are the perfect match for game meat, beef, poultry, and pork. The tangy, sweet, and mild flavor of maple pairs well with poultry, beef, and pork. Mesquite's tangy and spicy flavor is well-suited for all types of meats except fish. One of the most commonly used wood pellets is hickory. It's bacon-like aroma and taste bonds well with all types of meats. Beef, pork, and poultry can be paired with the spicy and nutty flavor of pecan wood chips.

Before you purchase any wood pellets, read through the list of ingredients to determine the percentage of flavor. Experiment with all these combinations to find something you love and enjoy. Allow your creativity and imagination to run wild as you experiment with different flavored wood pellets and meats.

Chapter 2:
Recipes for Rubs, Marinades, Sauces and Glaze

BBQ Rub Recipes

All-Purpose Dry Rub

Makes: About 1-1/3 cups

Ingredients:

- 4 tbsp paprika or 3 tbsp smoked paprika
- 2 tbsp freshly ground black pepper
- 2 tbsp chili powder
- 1 tbsp ground coriander
- 2 tbsp kosher salt
- 2 tbsp brown sugar
- 1 ½ tbsp ground cumin
- ½ tbsp cayenne pepper or to taste

Directions:

1. Combine all the spices, brown sugar, and salt in a bowl. Transfer into an airtight container.

BBQ Spice Rub

Makes: About 2/3 cup

Ingredients:

- ¼ cup brown sugar
- ½ tbsp ground black pepper
- ½ tbsp chili powder
- ½ tbsp onion powder
- ¼ cup paprika
- ½ tbsp salt
- ½ tbsp garlic powder
- ½ tsp cayenne pepper

Directions:

1. Combine all the spices, brown sugar, and salt in a bowl. Transfer into an airtight container.

Cajun Dry Rub

Makes: About 1-½ cups

Ingredients:

- 6 tbsp paprika
- 2 tbsp garlic flakes
- 2 tbsp ground white pepper
- 2 tbsp ground black pepper
- 1 tsp cayenne
- 2 tbsp onion flakes
- 1 tbsp dried thyme
- 1 tbsp dried oregano
- 6 tbsp kosher salt
- ½ tsp ground bay leaves
- 2 tbsp brown sugar
- ½ tbsp file powder

Directions:

1. Combine all the spices, dried herbs, and salt in a bowl. Transfer into an airtight container.

Basic Beef Rub

Makes: About 1 ¼ cups

Ingredients:

- ½ cup kosher salt
- 1 ½ tbsp granulated garlic
- ½ cup coarsely grounded black pepper
- 1 tsp ground red pepper

Directions:

1. Combine garlic, black pepper, red pepper, and salt in a bowl. Transfer into an airtight container.

Basic Pork Rub

Makes: About 1-¾ cups

Ingredients:

- 2/3 cup paprika
- ¼ cup ground black pepper
- ¼ cup salt
- 4 tsp chili powder
- 1 tsp cayenne pepper
- ½ cup sugar
- 2 tsp ground white pepper
- 4 tsp dry mustard

Directions:

1. Combine all the spices, sugar, and salt in a bowl. Transfer into an airtight container.

Pulled Pork Rub

Makes: Slightly less than 2 cups

Ingredients:

- ½ cup paprika
- ¼ cup ground black pepper
- 6 tbsp salt
- 2 tbsp cayenne pepper
- ½ cup brown sugar
- 4 tsp dry mustard

Directions:

1. Combine all the spices, brown sugar, and salt in a bowl. Transfer into an airtight container.

Easy Brisket Rub

Makes: About 2-½ cups

Ingredients:

- 4 tbsp salt
- 2 tbsp coarsely ground black pepper
- 2/3 cup paprika
- 6 tbsp garlic powder
- 4 tbsp dried oregano
- 2/3 cup brown sugar
- 6 tbsp onion powder

Directions:

1. Combine all the spices, brown sugar, oregano, and salt in a bowl. Transfer into an airtight container.

Dry Chimichurri Steak Rub

Makes: About 2/3 cup

Ingredients:

- 3 tbsp sea salt
- ½ tsp coarsely ground black pepper
- ½ tsp red pepper flakes
- 2 tbsp paprika
- 2 tsp garlic powder
- 2 tbsp dried oregano
- 2 tsp red pepper flakes
- 2 tbsp granulated onion

Directions:

1. Combine all the spices, basil, oregano, and salt in a bowl. Transfer into an airtight container.
2. Use as required.
3. To use it as a wet rub, add juice of four limes into the mixture of spices along with ½ cup of oil just before using the rub. Stir the mixture until well combined and use it on the meat.

Steak Dry Rub

Makes: ½ cup

Ingredients:

- 1-½ tbsp salt
- 1 tbsp coarsely ground black pepper
- ½ tbsp ground cumin
- 1-½ tbsp smoked paprika

- 1 tbsp garlic powder
- 1 tbsp dried oregano
- ½ tbsp light brown sugar
- 1 tbsp onion powder

Directions:

1. Combine all the spices, brown sugar, oregano, and salt in a bowl. Transfer into an airtight container.

Chili Lime Wet Rub

Makes: About ¾ cup

Ingredients:

- 4 tbsp kosher salt
- 2 tbsp chili powder
- 2 tsp dried cilantro
- 1 tsp garlic powder
- 2 tbsp finely chopped lime zest
- 1 tbsp smoked paprika
- 1 tsp onion powder
- 6 tbsp olive oil

Directions:

1. Combine all the spices, lime zest, cilantro and salt in a bowl.
2. Stir in the oil. Cover the bowl and chill until use.

Wet Rub (For any type of meat)

Makes: About 1-¾ cups

Ingredients:

- 2 tbsp paprika
- 2 tbsp cayenne
- 2 tbsp thyme
- 1 tbsp onion powder
- 4 tbsp dark beer
- 2 tbsp bourbon
- 2 tbsp ground black pepper
- 2 tbsp lemon pepper
- 2 tbsp sea salt
- 4 tbsp brown sugar
- 2 tbsp honey
- 2 tbsp lime juice

Directions:

1. Combine all the spices, thyme, and salt in a bowl.

2. Stir in the beer, bourbon, honey, and lime juice.

3. To use: Smear the rub mixture over the meat. Wrap the meat in cling wrap. Chill for an hour before grilling if possible.

Ancho Wet Rub for Steaks

Makes: About 1-½ cups

Ingredients:

- 8 dried Ancho chilies
- ¼ cup fresh cilantro
- 4 tbsp lime juice
- 6 cloves garlic, peeled
- 4 tsp salt
- 4 tbsp oil of your choice

Directions:

1. Place ancho chilies in a bowl. Pour boiling water over it. Let it soak for 15 minutes.
2. Drain off the water. Discard stems and seeds and place them in a blender.
3. Add garlic, cilantro, lime juice, salt, and oil and blend until you get a fine paste.
4. To use: Smear the rub mixture over the meat. Wrap the meat in cling wrap. Chill for four–eight hours before grilling if possible.

Perfect Smoked Chicken Rub

Makes: About ½ cup

Ingredients:

- 8 tsp salt
- 2 tsp onion powder
- 2 tsp dried thyme
- 1 tsp cayenne pepper (optional)
- 4 tsp smoked paprika
- 2 tsp garlic powder
- 2 tsp ground white pepper

- 1 tsp ground black pepper

Directions:

1. Combine all the spices, thyme, and salt in a bowl. Transfer into an airtight container.

BBQ Chicken Rub

Makes: 1-1/8 cups

Ingredients:

- ½ cup brown sugar
- 2 tbsp chili powder
- 4 tsp garlic powder
- ½ tsp finely crushed dried oregano
- 6 tsp salt
- 2 tsp onion powder
- 6 tsp sweet paprika

Directions:

1. Combine all the spices, brown sugar, oregano, and salt in a bowl. Transfer into an airtight container.

Chipotle Chicken Wet Rub

Makes: About ½ cup

Ingredients:

- 4 tbsp olive oil
- 1 tsp chili powder
- 2 tsp chipotle chili powder

- 1 tsp garlic powder
- 1 tsp onion powder
- 1 tsp salt
- 1 tsp smoked paprika
- 1 tsp ground cumin
- 2 tbsp lemon juice

Directions:

1. Combine all the spices, oil, lemon juice, and salt in a bowl.

2. Rub this mixture all over the chicken. Let it rest for 30–40 minutes on your countertop before grilling. You can also place it in a refrigerator for seven–eight hours if desired. If chilling the chicken, let it come to room temperature before grilling.

Sweet Rub for Grilled Pork and Chicken

Makes: About 1-1/3 cups

Ingredients:

- ½ cup dark brown sugar
- 4 tsp cracked black pepper
- 4 tsp garlic powder
- 2 tsp ground mustard
- 2 tbsp coarse sea salt
- 4 tsp smoked paprika
- 4 tsp onion powder
- 1 tsp cayenne pepper

Directions:

1. Combine all the spices, brown sugar, oregano, and salt in a bowl. Transfer into an airtight container.

Herbs Spice Rub For Poultry

Makes: ½ cup

Ingredients:

- 2 tbsp dried crushed parsley
- 2 tbsp dried crushed rosemary
- 2 tbsp dried crushed oregano
- 2 tbsp dried crushed bay leaves
- 4 tbsp dried crushed sage
- 2 tbsp dried crushed thyme
- 2 tbsp dried crushed basil
- 2 tbsp sugar
- 2 tbsp ground black pepper

Directions:

1. Combine all the dried herbs, sugar, and pepper in a spice blender. Process until finely powdered. Transfer into an airtight container.

2. To brine: Apply salt (only if required i.e. if meat is not salted) on the meat a day before grilling, if the meat is thick cut. If the meat is thin cut, apply salt on the meat a couple of hours before grilling.

3. You can use this rub on potatoes and asparagus as well. Brush meat or potatoes or asparagus with water. Sprinkle a generous amount of rub on the meat and place it in the refrigerator for an hour if possible. Cook it on your grill.

Smoked Turkey Rub

Makes: Around 1/3 cup

Ingredients:

- 1-½ tbsp brown sugar
- 1 tbsp kosher salt
- ½ tbsp garlic powder
- 1 tbsp smoked paprika
- ½ tbsp ground black pepper
- ½ tbsp onion powder
- ½ tsp dried thyme
- ¼ tsp celery salt
- ½ tsp crushed rosemary
- ¼ tsp rubbed sage
- 1/8 tsp cayenne pepper

Directions:

1. Combine all the spices, brown sugar, dried herbs, and salt in a bowl. Transfer into an airtight container.

Texas Style Rub

Makes: 1/3 cup

Ingredients:

- 1 tbsp crushed black peppercorns
- ½ tsp cayenne pepper
- ½ tbsp brown sugar
- 1 tbsp chili powder
- 1 tbsp garlic powder

- 1 tbsp kosher salt
- ½ tbsp paprika
- 1 tsp ground ginger
- 1 tbsp onion powder

Directions:

1. Combine all the spices, brown sugar and salt in a bowl.
2. Transfer into an airtight container.

Citrus and Herb Butter Wet Rub for Poultry

Makes: About ½ cup

Ingredients:

- ¼ cup unsalted butter, at room temperature
- Zest of ½ lemon, grated
- Zest of an orange, grated
- 2 tbsp minced fresh sage
- 1-½ tbsp minced fresh thyme
- 2 tbsp minced fresh rosemary
- ¼ tsp salt
- 2 cloves garlic, minced
- ¼ tsp freshly cracked pepper

Directions:

1. Combine butter, zests, fresh herbs, salt, garlic, and pepper in a bowl.
2. To use: Rub the herb butter all over the meat. Season the meat with salt and pepper.
3. Roast or grill the meat.

Dry Lamb Rub

Makes: About 1 1/8 cups

Ingredients:

- 4 tbsp dried rosemary leaves, crushed
- 1 tbsp dried ground bay leaves
- 2 tbsp ground black pepper
- 4 tbsp mustard seeds
- 2 tbsp paprika
- 20 cloves garlic, peeled, minced

Directions:

1. Combine all the spices and rosemary in a bowl. Transfer into an airtight container.

2. To brine: Apply salt (only if required i.e. if meat is not salted) on the meat a day before grilling, if the meat is thick cut. If the meat is thin cut, apply salt on the meat a couple of hours before grilling.

3. Rub the spice mixture over the meat. It is best to grill after at least two–three hours after applying the rub.

4. To use it as wet rub, add a few tablespoons of water and mix well. Apply the rub on the meat and you can grill it immediately.

Texas-style Lamb Dry Rub

Makes: About 1-½ cups

Ingredients:

- 2 tbsp whole coriander seeds
- 2 tbsp cumin seeds
- 2 tbsp yellow mustard seeds
- 2 tbsp brown sugar

- 2 tbsp chili powder
- 2 tbsp garlic powder
- 1 ¼ tbsp black pepper
- 2 tbsp paprika
- 4 tbsp sea salt
- 2 tbsp onion powder
- 2 tbsp dried oregano

Directions:

1. Place a skillet over medium flame. Let the skillet heat for a couple of minutes.

2. Add cumin seeds, mustard seeds and mustard seeds and stir constantly until you get a nice aroma and the seeds are light golden brown in color. Turn off the heat and cool for a few minutes.

3. Transfer the spices into a spice blender and grind into a fine powder.

4. Add the ground spices into a bowl. Add rest of the powdered spices, salt, brown sugar and oregano and stir until well combined.

5. To use: Rub this mixture all over the lamb, about eight hours before grilling. Cover the meat and place in the refrigerator.

Marinade Recipes

Pork Chop Marinade

Makes: About 2 cups

Ingredients:

- 1 cup extra-virgin olive oil
- ½ cup brown sugar
- 4 cloves garlic, peeled, minced
- 8 tbsp apple cider vinegar
- 4 tbsp grainy mustard
- 1 tsp red pepper flakes
- 2 tsp salt or to taste
- Freshly ground pepper to taste

Directions:

1. Combine oil, brown sugar, garlic, pepper, vinegar, mustard, red pepper flakes and salt in a bowl.

2. To use: Place pork in the bowl. Turn the pork around in the bowl, to coat well. Chill for two–four hours before grilling the pork.

Chicken Marinade

Makes: 2–2 ¼ cups

Ingredients:

- 2/3–1 cup extra-virgin olive oil
- 6 tbsp soy sauce
- 6 tbsp fresh lemon juice
- 4 tbsp balsamic vinegar
- 2 tbsp Worcestershire sauce
- 3 tsp salt
- ½ cup brown sugar
- 6 cloves garlic, peeled, minced
- 2 tsp pepper

Directions:

1. Combine oil, soy sauce, brown sugar, garlic, pepper, lemon juice, balsamic vinegar, Worcestershire sauce and salt in a bowl.

2. To use: Score the chicken lightly. Place chicken in the bowl. Turn the chicken around in the bowl to coat well. Grill after two–four hours.

Spicy Asian Chicken Wing Marinade

Makes: 1-2/3 cups

Ingredients:

- 2/3 cup extra-virgin olive oil
- 4 tbsp honey
- 6 tbsp low-sodium soy sauce
- 2 tbsp fresh lime juice
- 2 tbsp chili garlic sauce
- 2 tbsp minced ginger
- 8 cloves garlic, peeled, minced

Directions:

1. Combine oil, soy sauce, ginger, garlic, lime juice, chili garlic sauce and honey in a bowl.

2. To use: Set aside about ¾ cup of the marinade. Place chicken in the bowl. Turn the chicken around in the bowl to coat well.

3. Keep the bowl covered, in the refrigerator for two hours.

4. Pour retained marinade in a small saucepan. Place the saucepan over medium flame and cook until thick.

5. Grill for a couple of minutes on each side. Baste the chicken with the retained, thickened marinade and continue grilling until chicken is well cooked inside and golden brown on the outside.

Tandoori Marinade

Makes: About 1-1/3 cups

Ingredients:

- 1 cup Greek yogurt
- 1 tbsp ginger paste
- 1 tbsp garlic paste
- 2 tsp Kashmiri chili powder or low heat chili powder
- 2 tsp kasuri methi (dried fenugreek leaves)
- 3 tbsp oil or your choice + extra to baste

- 2 tsp Tandoori chicken masala or garam masala (Indian spice blends)
- 2 tsp ground coriander
- ½ tsp crushed black pepper
- ½ tsp salt
- 2 tbsp lemon juice + extra to serve
- ½ tsp turmeric powder

Directions:

1. Combine all the spices and salt in a bowl. Add Greek yogurt, ginger paste, garlic paste, oil and lemon juice and stir until well combined.

2. To use on chicken: Score the chicken and place chicken in the bowl. Turn the chicken around in the bowl to coat well.

3. Keep the bowl covered, in the refrigerator for six–eight hours. The longer it marinates the better. Ideal time is eight hours.

4. Remove the bowl from the refrigerator an hour before grilling.

5. Baste with oil while grilling.

6. Drizzle lemon juice over the grilled chicken.

7. This marinade can also be used on potatoes or cauliflower or paneer (a type of cottage cheese). If you are using potatoes or cauliflower, parboil the vegetables before marinating.

Cuban Mojo Marinade for Pork

Makes: About 1-½ cups

Ingredients:

- 6 tbsp extra-virgin olive oil

- 6 tbsp fresh orange juice
- ½ tbsp grated orange zest
- ¼ cup fresh lime juice
- 1/8 cup mint leaves
- ½ tbsp minced fresh oregano or 1 tsp dried oregano
- Salt to taste
- ½ cup fresh cilantro leaves
- Pepper to taste
- 4 cloves garlic, peeled, smashed
- ½ tsp ground cumin

Directions:

1. Place cilantro, garlic, mint and orange juice in a blender and give short pulses until finely chopped. You can also finely chop the garlic, mint and cilantro and mix it with orange juice.

2. Transfer the mixture into a Ziploc bag. Also add orange zest, lime juice, oregano and cumin. Seal the bag and shake until well combined.

3. To use: Place pork in the bag and turn the bag around so that pork is well coated with the marinade. Place the bag in a dish and chill for eight–nine hours.

4. Remove only pork from the bag and grill it. The marinade is to be discarded.

Chapter 3:
Pork Recipes

Smoked Country Style Ribs with Texas Rub

Preparation time: 40 minutes

Cooking time: 4 hours

Cooking method: Smoking

Makes: 3 servings

Temperature: 225°F

Pellets: Hickory or apple

Ingredients:

- 1/3 cup Texas rub

- 4 country style pork ribs
- Dijon mustard or spicy brown mustard, as required

Directions:

1. Smear mustard all over the ribs. Sprinkle Texas rub all over. Press lightly to adhere the rub over the ribs.

2. Chill for about 30 minutes.

3. Operate the grill following the instructions of the manufacturer and light up the pellets. Set the grill on the 'Smoke' option. Leave the lid open and let it operate for 10 minutes. Set the temperature at 225°F and preheat the grill.

4. Lay the ribs on the grates. Keep the lid closed. Set the timer for 3-½–4 hours. When the timer goes off, check the internal temperature of the ribs.

5. When the ribs are cooked through inside, the internal temperature should be 185°F. It is now time to take out the ribs. Let it rest for 10 minutes before serving.

Smoked Baby Back Ribs with Bourbon Glaze

Preparation time: 15 minutes + chilling time

Cooking time: 2–3 hours

Cooking method: Grilling

Makes: 8 servings

Temperature: 300°F

Pellets: Hickory or maple or apple

Ingredients:

- 4–4-½ lbs baby back rib
- 2 cups bourbon glaze
- 1 tsp ground cinnamon
- 2 sticks cinnamon
- 3 tsp dry mustard
- 12 thin strips peeled ginger
- 2 large onions, sliced
- 2 tsp ground ginger
- 2 tbsp coarse kosher salt
- 3 tsp dried thyme
- 1 tsp cayenne pepper
- 2 tbsp apple cider

Directions:

1. Combine dry mustard thyme, dry mustard, ground ginger, cayenne, ground cinnamon and salt in a bowl.

2. Sprinkle the spice rub on both the sides of the rib rack and place it in a roasting pan and cover the pan.

3. Place the pan in the refrigerator for six–24 hours depending on how much time you have on hand.

4. Operate the grill following the instructions of the manufacturer and light up the pellets. Set the grill on 'Smoke' option. Leave the lid open and let it operate for 10 minutes. Set the temperature at 300°F and close the lid to preheat the grill.

5. Take out the roasting pan from the refrigerator and pick up the rib rack from the pan. Place onion slices on the bottom of the pan. Scatter the cinnamon sticks and ginger slices over the onions.

6. Drizzle apple cider over onions. Place the ribs back in the pan with the meat side touching the onions. Keep the pan covered with aluminum foil and place it in the smoking case.

7. Close the lid and roast until the meat is well cooked and is coming off the bones. It should take two–three hours.

8. Remove the foil and let it cool for 30–40 minutes.

9. Raise the temperature of the grill to 400°F. Shift ribs directly on the grill grate and set 'Grill' option and timer for about 12–13 minutes.

10. Grill for five minutes on each side. Now brush the bourbon glaze generously all over the ribs and grill for three minutes on either side.

11. Remove the ribs from the grill and place them on your cutting board. Slice between the bones and serve.

Hot Dogs Wrapped in Bacon

Preparation time: 2 minutes

Cooking time: 10 minutes

Cooking method: Grilling

Makes: 3 servings

Temperature: 350°F – 450°F

Pellets: Apple or cherry

Ingredients:

- 3 hot dogs
- 3 hot dog buns, split
- 3 strips bacon
- 1 tbsp vegetable oil
- 1 green bell pepper, diced

- Pit Boss Smoke Infused Applewood Bacon Rub, as required

Directions:

1. Operate the grill following the instructions of the manufacturer and light up the pellets. Set the temperature at 350°F–450°F and close the lid to preheat the grill.

2. Grease the grill grates with oil using a cloth

3. Wrap a strip of bacon over each hot dog. Fasten with a toothpick at the ends.

4. Place the hotdogs on the grill and cook until bacon is slightly crisp. This should be done in four to six minutes depending on the temperature you have set.

5. Remove the hot dogs from the grill.

6. Now place the hot dog buns on the grill and set the broiler option. Toast the buns to the desired crispiness.

7. Place the hot dogs on the bottom half of the buns. Top with bell pepper. Cover the sandwiches with the top half of the buns and serve.

Chapter 4:
Beef Recipes

Hot and Fast Beef Brisket

Preparation time: 60 minutes

Cooking time: 30 minutes per pound of meat

Cooking method: Grilling

Makes: 4–5 servings

Temperature: 300°F

Pellets: Hickory or oak or mesquite

Ingredients:

- 6–8 lbs whole packer cut brisket, fat cap trimmed
- ¼ cup beef broth

- 2 tbsp coarse black pepper
- 1 tbsp minced fresh rosemary
- 1 tbsp celery seed powder
- 2 tbsp kosher salt

Directions:

1. Operate the grill following the instructions of the manufacturer and light up the pellets. Set the grill on 'Smoke' option. Leave the lid open and let it operate for 10 minutes. Set the temperature at 300°F and preheat the grill, with the lid closed.

2. Meanwhile, mix together all the spices, salt and rosemary in a bowl. Sprinkle the rub all over the brisket and massage the spice mixture into the brisket.

3. Lay the brisket in the center of the grill, making sure to keep the fat side facing down, touching the grill. Keep the lid closed.

4. Check the temperature after about 1-½ to two hours. When the internal temperature of the brisket is 165°F, remove the brisket from the grill wearing gloves and keep it on your cutting board.

5. Take a large sheet of aluminum foil and pour two tablespoons of broth on the center of the foil. Place the brisket on it and wrap the foil tightly, all over the brisket. Make sure not to wrap the brisket before the internal temperature is 165°F.

6. Place it back on the grill. Continue cooking until the internal temperature of the meat is 195°F–205°F. Check the temperature every 30–40 minutes.

7. When you are satisfied with the cooking, take out the brisket from the grill and place it on your cutting board. Open a bit of the foil to remove some steam. Close the opened bit once again and seal it well.

8. Now wrap the entire brisket (along with foil) with a towel. Place it in a cooler for an hour.

9. Unwrap and cut into slices, against the grain.

Smoked Brisket

Preparation time: 15 minutes + chilling time

Cooking time: About 1-½ hours per lb of meat

Cooking method: Smoking

Makes: 5–6 servings

Temperature: 250°F–260°F

Pellets: Hickory, oak or pecan

Ingredients:

- 6–7 lbs beef brisket, trimmed
- ½ cup easy brisket rub or basic beef rub
- 4 tbsp Worcestershire sauce
- BBQ sauce to serve, as required

Directions:

1. Brush Worcestershire sauce all over the brisket.

2. Sprinkle rub all over the brisket and place it on a tray. Refrigerate for one–four hours

3. Operate the grill following the instructions of the manufacturer and light up the pellets. Set the grill on 'Smoke' option. Leave the lid open and let it operate for 10 minutes. Set the temperature between 250°F–260°F and preheat for about 25–30 minutes, keeping the lid closed.

4. Place a drip pan on the bottom shelf.

5. Place meat on the top grill grate. Close the lid. Cook for about two–three hours or until a meat thermometer when inserted in the thickest portion of the meat shows 165°F. Remove the meat from the grill and wrap it tightly with butcher paper. Keep it back on the grill and continue smoking until the internal temperature of the meat shows 200°F.

6. Remove the butcher paper and let it rest for three–four minutes. Cover it loosely with butcher paper. Let it rest for two hours.

7. Slice the brisket into ¼ inch thick slices across the grain.

8. Serve with BBQ sauce.

Juicy Cheeseburger

Preparation time: 25 minutes

Cooking time: 5–8 minutes per side

Cooking method: Grilling

Makes: 8 servings

Temperature: 200°F

Pellets: Apple or cherry

Ingredients:

<u>For burger:</u>

- 4 lbs ground beef
- 2 cups dry breadcrumbs
- 2 eggs, beaten
- 6 tbsp evaporated milk
- 2 tbsp basic beef rub or any other rub of your choice
- 5 slices cheddar cheese

To serve:

- 8 burger buns, split
- Extra cheese (optional)
- Any other toppings of your choice

Directions:

1. Combine ground beef, evaporated milk, eggs, rub and Worcestershire sauce in a bowl, using your hands.

2. Make 16 equal portions of the mixture and shape them into thin patties. The size of the patties should be slightly bigger than the diameter of the burger buns.

3. Line a baking sheet with parchment paper. Place eight of the patties over it. Place a slice of cheese on each patty.

4. Place a patty over each cheese slice. So now you have a cheese slice sandwiched between two patties which is one burger and eight burgers in all. Press the patties at the edges together to seal.

5. Operate the grill following the instructions of the manufacturer and light up the pellets. Set the grill on 'Grill' option. Set the temperature at 300°F and close the lid to preheat the grill.

6. Place the burgers on the grill grate and grill for five–eight minutes. Flip sides and grill the other side for six–eight minutes.

7. Remove the burgers and place them on a plate.

8. Place the burger buns on the grill and toast them to the desired doneness.

9. Place burgers on the bottom half of the buns. Place desired toppings over the burgers. Cover with the top half of the buns and serve.

Espresso Coriander Rubbed Beef Tenderloin

Preparation time: 5 minutes

Cooking time: 1 hour

Cooking method: Grilling

Makes: 4 servings

Temperature: 425°F

Pellets: Cherry

Ingredients:

- 1 (2 lbs) whole beef tenderloin, at room temperature, trimmed of excess fat and silverskin
- ½ tbsp brown sugar

- 1/8 tsp ground cayenne pepper
- ¼ tsp sea salt
- ½ tsp finely diced chives
- 1 tbsp ground espresso
- 1 tsp ground coriander
- ¼ tsp garlic powder
- ½ tbsp grated lemon zest
- 1 tbsp olive oil
- Freshly ground black pepper

Directions:

1. Operate the grill following the instructions of the manufacturer and light up the pellets. Set the grill on 'Grill' option. Set the temperature at 425°F and close the lid to preheat the grill.

2. Insert the thin end of the tenderloin below itself and tie up the tenderloin with a kitchen string.

3. To make rub: Stir together in a bowl, espresso, chives, lemon zest, sugar, salt and all the spices.

4. Brush oil all over the tenderloin. Sprinkle the rub over the tenderloin. Rub it well into it.

5. Place meat on the grill grate and cook until a meat thermometer when inserted in the thickest portion of the meat shows 130°F.

6. Wrap the tenderloin with foil and place it on your cutting board, to rest for 15 minutes.

7. Untie the meat and slice and serve with a side dish of your choice.

Chapter 5:
Lamb Recipes

Smoked Leg of Lamb with Fennel, Rosemary, Garlic Rub

Preparation time: 15 minutes + chilling time

Cooking time: About 30 minutes per lb of meat

Cooking method: Smoking

Makes: 4 servings

Temperature: 425°F

Pellets: Competition blend

Ingredients:

- 3–4 lbs leg of lamb
- 2–3 cloves garlic, peeled, slivered
- Lemon pepper garlic and herb seasoning to taste
- 1–2 tbsp toasted, ground fennel seeds
- Few rosemary sprigs, cut into 1 inch pieces

Directions:

1. Sprinkle fennel powder all over the meat and rub it well into it. Sprinkle a generous amount of lemon pepper garlic and herb seasoning over the meat.

2. Take a paring knife and pierce holes on the outermost surface of the meat. The holes should be an inch deep. Distance between two holes should be 1–1-½ inches.

3. Place the rosemary and garlic slices in these holes.

4. Place the meat in a bowl and chill for four–eight hours. Do not cover the meat in the refrigerator.

5. Set the grill on 'Smoke' option. Leave the lid open and let it operate for 10 minutes. Set the temperature to 180°F and preheat for about 15 minutes.

6. Smoke the meat for about one hour.

7. Increase the temperature of the grill to 425°F and cook until a golden brown colored crust forms on top.

8. Lower the temperature of the grill to 325°F and cook until the internal temperature of the meat is 125°F.

9. Take out the meat from the grill and tent it loosely with foil. Let it sit for 15 minutes.

10. Slice and serve.

Smoked Lamb Sausage

Preparation time: 2 hours

Cooking time: 1 hour and 10 minutes

Cooking method: Smoking

Makes: 8–9 servings

Temperature: 225°F, 500°F

Pellets: Cherry

Ingredients:

For sausage:

- 3 lbs lamb shoulder, cut into 2 inch pieces
- 1-½ tsp ground cumin
- ¾ tsp cayenne pepper

- 2 tbsp finely chopped parsley
- 2 tbsp finely chopped cilantro
- 1-½ tsp ground black pepper
- 1-½ tbsp minced garlic
- 1-½ tsp paprika
- 3 tbsp ground fennel
- 3 tbsp salt

For yogurt and cucumber sauce:
- 4-½ cups Greek yogurt
- 2 cloves garlic, peeled, minced
- 2 tbsp finely chopped dill
- Ground black pepper to taste
- 2 tbsp lemon juice or to taste
- 2 cucumbers, peeled, grated
- Salt to taste

Directions:

1. Grind the lamb pieces in a meat grinder. Transfer into a bowl. Add all the spices and salt and mix well. Chill for about two hours.

2. Fix the hog casing with the help of a sausage horn to the grinder. Fill the grinder with sausage and fill up the casing with sausage. Turn and twist the sausage along with casing every few inches to make sausage links.

3. Once the links have been made, pierce with a fork on the casing at a few places on each of the links. This is done to release steam during cooking. Place the sausage links in the refrigerator.

4. To make yogurt and cucumber sauce: Combine Greek yogurt, garlic, dill, pepper, lemon juice, cucumber and salt in a bowl. Cover and chill until use.

5. Operate the grill following the instructions of the manufacturer and light up the pellets. Set the grill on 'Smoke' option. Leave the lid open and let it operate for 10 minutes. Set the temperature to 225°F and preheat for about 15 minutes.

6. Smoke the sausages for about one hour.

7. Take out the links from the grill and set it aside on a plate.

8. Increase the temperature of the grill to 500°F. Close the lid and preheat the grill.

9. Keep the sausage links on the grill once again and cook for five minutes. Turn the sausages and cook the other side for five minutes.

10. Remove the sausages from the grill and serve with yogurt and cucumber sauce with a side dish of your choice.

Braised Lamb Shoulder Tacos

Preparation time: 15 minutes + few hours or resting

Cooking time: 5 hours

Cooking method: Grilling

Makes: 8 servings

Temperature: 225°F

Pellets: Big game blend

Ingredients:

- 6 lbs lamb shoulders
- ½ tbsp cumin seeds
- ½ tbsp pumpkin seeds
- ½ tbsp coriander seeds
- 4 oz guajillo peppers, deseeded
- 2 tbsp lime juice
- 6 cloves garlic, peeled
- 2 tbsp salt
- 2 tbsp chopped fresh oregano
- 2 tbsp smoked paprika
- 4 tbsp olive oil

To serve:

- Tortillas
- Pickled radishes
- Lime juice
- Any other toppings of your choice
- Cilantro

Directions:

1. Place cumin seeds, pumpkin seeds and coriander seeds in the spice grinder and grind into a fine powder.

2. Place guajillo chilies in a bowl (microwave safe) of water. The chilies should be just covered with water.

3. Cook on high in a microwave for two minutes. Once it cools slightly, remove chilies from the bowl and place in a blender. Also add ¼ cup of the soaked water, powdered seeds, lime juice, garlic, olive oil, paprika, oregano and salt and blend until smooth.

4. Place lamb in a roasting pan. Pour about a cup of sauce over the lamb and rub it into it. Place it on your countertop for two–12 hours.

62

5. Operate the grill following the instructions of the manufacturer and light up the pellets. Set the grill on 'Grill' option. Set the temperature to 325°F and preheat for about 15 minutes. Keep the lid closed while preheating.

6. Pour about a cup of water into the roasting pan and keep the pan covered loosely, with foil.

7. Place the lamb in the grill and cook for about 2-½ hours. Add water into the pan as and when required. Keep checking every 40–50 minutes.

8. Uncover and continue cooking until lamb is cooked through. Drizzle the cooked liquid over the lamb occasionally.

9. Take out the lamb from the grill and let it rest for about 30 minutes.

10. Shred the meat with a pair of forks and mix into the cooked liquid.

11. Serve hot over tortillas drizzled, with lime juice. Place any toppings if desired along with pickled radishes and serve.

Chapter 6:
Poultry Recipes

Smoked Turkey

Preparation time: 20 minutes + chilling time

Cooking time: 30–40 minutes per pound of meat

Cooking method: Smoking

Makes: 4 servings

Temperature: 180°F, 350°F

Pellets: Pecan

Ingredients:

- 1 fresh or frozen turkey (10–12 lbs), thawed if frozen, remove giblets
- 1 tbsp minced garlic
- 1/3 cup Worcestershire sauce
- ¾ cup smoked turkey rub or any other poultry rub of your choice
- ¾ cup sugar
- 1-½ tbsp canola oil

Directions:

1. Take a non-metal bucket and pour about 2–2-½ gallons of water into the bucket.

2. Stir garlic, sugar, turkey rub and Worcestershire sauce into the bucket. This is the brine.

3. Lay the turkey in the brine, with the breast side facing down. The turkey should be immersed in the brine so add more water if required.

4. Keep the bucket covered and in the refrigerator for eight–nine hours.

5. Take out the bucket from the refrigerator and the turkey from the brine. Dry it by patting with paper towels.

6. Rub oil all over the turkey and place it in the disposable aluminum roasting pan, this time make sure that the breast side is facing up.

7. Operate the grill following the instructions of the manufacturer and light up the pellets. Set the grill on 'Smoke' option. Leave the lid open and let it operate for 10 minutes. Set the temperature to 225°F and preheat for about 15 minutes, with the lid closed.

8. Place the roasting pan on the grill and set the timer for about 2–2-½ hours. When the timer goes off, raise the temperature of the grill to 350°F.

9. Continue cooking until the internal temperature of the meat in the thickest part is 165°F. Check the temperature every 30–40 minutes.

10. When you are satisfied with the cooking, take out the turkey from the grill and place it on your cutting board.

11. Let it rest for about 30 minutes.

12. Slice and serve with a side dish.

Barbecue Turkey Legs

Preparation time: 10 minutes

Cooking time: 2 hours

Cooking method: Smoke

Makes: 3–4 servings

Temperature: 225°F, 325°F

Pellets: Hickory or maple or mesquite

Ingredients:

- 1 tsp ground black pepper
- ¼ tsp cayenne pepper

- 1 tsp granulated garlic
- ½ tbsp kosher salt
- ½ tbsp brown sugar
- 1 tsp ground coriander
- 2 lbs turkey drumsticks
- 1 tbsp olive oil

Directions:

1. Operate the grill following the instructions of the manufacturer and light up the pellets. Set the grill on 'Smoke' option. Leave the lid open and let it operate for 10 minutes. Set the temperature at 225°F and preheat the grill.

2. Lay the turkey legs on a baking sheet. Brush them with olive oil.

3. Combine all the spices, salt and brown sugar in a bowl. Sprinkle this mixture all over the turkey legs and place the baking sheet in the smoking case and close the lid.

4. Set the timer for 1-½ hours. When the timer goes off, check the internal temperature of the legs.

5. Raise the temperature of the grill to 325°F. Shift the turkey legs to the lower grill grate and select the 'Grill' option and set the timer for about 25–30 minutes, making sure to turn the turkey legs every five minutes, after 20 minutes of grilling.

6. When the turkey legs are cooked through inside, the internal temperature of the meat when checked with a meat thermometer should be 170°F. It is now time to take out the turkey from the grill. Let it rest for 10 minutes before serving.

Hot and Fast BBQ Turkey

Preparation time: 30 minutes

Cooking time: 2 hours

Cooking method: Smoking

Makes: 6–7 servings

Temperature: 450°F

Pellets: Mesquite

Ingredients:

- 2 small bay leaves
- ¼ tsp chili flakes
- 3 tbsp honey
- 1 turkey, thawed
- 3 tbsp olive oil
- ¾ cup turkey stock
- 1-½ tbsp Worcestershire sauce

- ¼ tsp ground black pepper or to taste
- 3 cloves garlic, peeled, smashed
- 2/3 cup honey chipotle BBQ sauce or any other BBQ sauce
- ¾ tsp kosher salt or to taste
- 2 thyme sprigs
- 2 ½ cups water

Directions:

1. Dry the turkey by patting it with paper towels. Grease the rack of the roasting pan with some oil and place turkey on the rack.

2. Combine turkey stock, garlic, olive oil, Worcestershire sauce, honey, chili flakes, salt and pepper in a saucepan.

3. Stir in thyme and bay leaves. Place the saucepan on your stovetop over high flame.

4. When the mixture begins to boil, lower the flame and cook for five minutes. Turn off the heat and let it cool for about 20 minutes.

5. Strain the mixture and discard the solids. Pour the strained solution into a marinade injector.

6. Inject the solution all over the turkey. Also smear about two teaspoons of the solution on top of the turkey.

7. Pour water into the bottom of the roasting pan.

8. Operate the grill following the instructions of the manufacturer and light up the pellets. Set the grill on 'Smoke' option. Leave the lid open and let it operate for 10 minutes. Set the temperature at 450°F and preheat the grill.

9. Place the roasting pan on the grill and roast until the internal temperature of the meat in the thickest part is 165°F. It should take about 1-½–2 hours. Rotate the turkey every half hour.

10. Cover the turkey loosely after the initial 30 minutes of cooking. Brush BBQ over the turkey during the last 10 minutes of roasting.

11. Once cooked, take out the turkey from the grill and let it sit for 30 minutes.

12. Slice and serve.

BBQ Turkey Breast

Preparation time: 10 minutes

Cooking time: 3 hours

Cooking method: Grilling

Makes: 4 servings

Temperature: 275°F

Pellets: Apple or mesquite or cherry or fruitwood

Ingredients:

- 1 large boneless, skinless turkey breast half
- BBQ spice rub, as required
- 2 tbsp Dijon mustard

- 2 tbsp mayonnaise or more if required
- ¼ cup honey

Directions:

1. Dry the turkey breast half by patting with paper towels.

2. Spread mayonnaise all over the turkey breast half. Be generous.

3. Sprinkle BBQ spice rub all over the turkey breast half.

4. Operate the grill following the instructions of the manufacturer and light up the pellets. Set the grill on 'Smoke' option. Leave the lid open and let it operate for 10 minutes. Set the temperature at 275°F and preheat the grill for 15 minutes. Close the lid while preheating.

5. Lay the turkey breast half on the grill grate. Close the lid and cook for a couple of hours until the internal temperature of the meat, when checked with a meat thermometer, in the thickest part is 158°F. It should take about 1-½–2 hours. Turn the turkey every half hour.

6. Meanwhile, make the glaze by combining Dijon mustard, honey and some BBQ spice rub (3–4 tsp) in a saucepan.

7. Place the saucepan over medium flame and stir frequently until the mixture comes to a boil.

8. Lower the flame and cook until it is one third its original quantity. Turn off the heat.

9. When the internal temperature of the meat in the thickest part is 158°F (check it with the meat thermometer), brush the glaze on the meat and continue grilling until the internal temperature of the meat is 160°F.

10. Take out the turkey breast half from the grill and place on your cutting board. When cool enough to handle, cut into slices and serve.

Chapter 7:
Seafood Recipes

BBQ Roasted Salmon

Preparation time: 15 minutes

Cooking time: 15 minutes

Cooking method: Grilling

Makes: 2 servings

Temperature: 350°F

Pellets: Alder

Ingredients:

- 2 salmon fillets (6 oz each), skin-on
- 3 tbsp honey
- ½ cup ketchup
- ½ tsp apple cider vinegar
- Salt to taste
- 1-½ tbsp whole grain mustard
- ¼ cup dark brown sugar
- ¼ tsp finely chopped thyme leaves
- Freshly ground pepper to taste

Directions:

1. Combine honey, ketchup, apple cider vinegar, salt, mustard, brown sugar, thyme and pepper in a bowl. If you have the time, make this sauce mixture a day in advance.

2. Rub this sauce mixture on both sides of the salmon. Set aside the remaining sauce mixture.

3. Operate the grill following the instructions of the manufacturer and light up the pellets. Set the grill on 'Grill' option. Set the temperature at 350°F and preheat the grill for 15 minutes. Close the lid while preheating.

4. Place the salmon on the grill grate and set the timer for 15 minutes.

5. Once grilled, remove the salmon from the grill and let it rest for three minutes.

6. Serve salmon with remaining sauce mixture.

Honey Smoked Salmon

Preparation time: 20 minutes + chilling time

Cooking time: 1 hour

Cooking method: Smoking

Makes: 4 servings

Temperature: 200°F

Pellets: Mesquite or maple or oak or competition

Ingredients:

- 3 cups brown sugar
- 4 tbsp cracked black pepper

- 4 tbsp minced garlic
- 4 tbsp lemon juice
- 2 tsp cayenne pepper
- 2 tbsp dill weed
- 6 tbsp honey
- Olive oil, as required
- 2 cups sea salt
- 4 large salmon fillets, scaled, deboned

Directions:

1. Stir together salt, brown sugar and all the spices in a large mixing bowl.
2. Dry the salmon by patting with paper towels. Brush the salmon with oil.
3. Dredge the salmon in the spice mixture and place on the baking sheet, with the skin side facing down.
4. Cover the salmon with another sheet of parchment paper. Chill for eight–nine hours.
5. Take out the baking sheet from the refrigerator. Rinse the salmon with cold water to remove the rub. Set it aside for a while.
6. Whisk together honey and lemon juice in a bowl. Brush a little of this mixture on the salmon fillets, on the flesh side.
7. Operate the grill following the instructions of the manufacturer and light up the pellets. Set the grill on 'Smoke' option. Leave the lid open and let it operate for 10 minutes.
8. Immerse the cedar plank in cold water for five minutes. Remove the plank from water and place it on the grill grate. Set the temperature at 250°F and preheat the grill for 15 minutes. Close the lid while preheating.
9. Place the salmon on the cedar plank and set the timer for 45 minutes.
10. Brush honey mixture once again on the salmon and continue smoking it for another 15–20 minutes. Once salmon is ready, you can see something white coming out from the salmon.
11. Remove the salmon from the grill and let it sit for 15 minutes.
12. Serve.

Roasted Sheet Pan Salmon with Spring Vegetables and Pesto

Preparation time: 10 minutes

Cooking time: 12 minutes

Cooking method: Grilling

Makes: 3 servings

Temperature: 500°F

Pellets: Apple

Ingredients:

- 3 salmons (4 oz each), skin-on, remove the pin bones

- Kosher salt to taste
- ½ lb sugar snap peas, trimmed, cut into ½ inch pieces on the diagonal
- ½ bunch asparagus, remove bottom third of the stalks, cut into 1 inch pieces
- 5 oz cherry tomatoes, halved
- 1-½ tbsp olive oil, divided
- Freshly ground black pepper to taste
- Zest of ½ lemon, grated
- 1 lemon, halved
- ¼ cup fresh pesto
- A handful fresh basil leaves, to garnish

Directions:

1. Operate the grill following the instructions of the manufacturer and light up the pellets. Set the grill on 'Grill' option. Set the temperature at 500°F and preheat the grill for 15 minutes. Close the lid while preheating.

2. Dry the salmon by patting with paper towels. Brush a little of the olive oil all over the salmon with a basting brush. Season with a generous amount of pepper and salt and place it on the lined baking sheet, making sure to leave at least two inches space between the salmons.

3. Combine snap peas, asparagus and cherry tomatoes in a bowl. Drizzle remaining oil over the vegetables. Sprinkle some salt and pepper and toss well.

4. Spread the vegetables all over the baking sheet.

5. Keep the baking sheet on the grill grate. Also place the lemon halves on the grill grate, in the front part of the lid. Set the timer for five minutes and keep the lid closed.

6. Take out the lemon halves from the grill. Give the vegetables a good stir and close the lid once again. Continue cooking for another five minutes or until fish is cooked through.

7. Drizzle pesto over the fish and vegetables. Squeeze juice from the grilled lemon and drizzle over the fish and vegetables.

8. Garnish with lemon zest and basil leaves and serve.

Chapter 8:
Appetizers and Sides Recipes

Parmesan Roasted Cauliflower

Preparation time: 20 minutes

Cooking time: 40 minutes

Cooking method: Grilling

Makes: 8 servings

Temperature: 400°F

Pellets: Pecan

Ingredients:

- 2 heads cauliflower, cut into florets
- 8 whole cloves garlic, unpeeled

- Salt to taste
- 2 tsp minced fresh thyme
- 2 medium onions, sliced
- 8 tbsp olive oil
- Ground black pepper to taste
- 1 cup grated parmesan cheese

Directions:

1. Operate the grill following the instructions of the manufacturer and light up the pellets. Set the grill on 'Grill' option. Set the temperature at 400°F and preheat the grill for 15 minutes. Close the lid while preheating.

2. Combine cauliflower, salt, pepper, onion, garlic, thyme and olive oil in a bowl.

3. Spread the cauliflower mixture on a baking sheet.

4. Place the baking sheet on the grill and roast the cauliflower until nearly tender. It should take around 20–25 minutes.

5. Sprinkle parmesan cheese over the cauliflower and continue roasting for some more time until cauliflower is now tender and the cheese is crisp.

6. Serve right away.

Smoked Deviled Eggs

Preparation time: 15 minutes

Cooking time: 30 hours

Cooking method: Grilling

Makes: 8 servings

Temperature: 180°F

Pellets: Hickory

Ingredients:

- 8 hard-boiled eggs, peeled
- 6 tsp finely chopped chives

- 2 tsp apple cider vinegar
- 6 tbsp mayonnaise
- 2 tsp brown mustard
- Hot sauce to taste
- ¼ cup cook, crumbled bacon
- Salt to taste
- Paprika to taste
- Pepper to taste

Directions:

1. Operate the grill following the instructions of the manufacturer and light up the pellets. Set the grill on 'Grill' option. Set the temperature at 180°F and preheat the grill for 15 minutes. Close the lid while preheating.

2. Lay the peeled eggs on the grill grate. Close the lid and set the timer for 30 minutes.

3. Take out the eggs from the grill and place it on a plate. Let it cool completely.

4. Cut the eggs into two halves along the length.

5. Carefully remove the egg yolks and place in a bowl. Mash the egg yolks. Add chives, vinegar, salt, mayonnaise, mustard, hot sauce and pepper and mix well.

6. Spoon the yolk mixture into a piping bag and pipe the mixture into the cavities of the whites. Place them on a serving platter.

7. Garnish with bacon and paprika and refrigerate until use.

Grilled Fruit Skewers with Yogurt Sauce

Preparation time: 30 minutes

Cooking time: 6 minutes

Cooking method: Grilling

Makes: 4 servings

Temperature: 275°F

Pellets: Apple

Ingredients:

- ½ cup water

- 2 tsp ground cinnamon
- 1 cup brown sugar
- Juice of an orange
- 4 nectarines, cut into 1 inch cubes
- 2 green apples, peeled, cut into 1 inch cubes
- 2 persimmons, cut into 1 inch cubes

For yogurt sauce:

- Juice of an orange
- 16 oz vanilla yogurt

Directions:

1. Place brown sugar, cinnamon, orange zest and water in a pot. Place the pot over medium flame over your stovetop. Stir often until brown sugar dissolves.

2. When it comes to a boil, turn off the heat and let it cool completely.

3. Operate the grill following the instructions of the manufacturer and light up the pellets. Set the grill on 'Grill' option. Set the temperature at 275°F and preheat the grill for 15 minutes. Close the lid while preheating.

4. Remove skewers from water. Thread the fruits on to the skewers, in any manner you like.

5. Place the skewers on the grill for six minutes. Turn the skewers slightly every 80–90 seconds, so that it grills evenly. Baste with the brown sugar syrup each time you turn the skewers.

6. To make yogurt sauce for dipping: Whisk together orange juice and yogurt in a bowl.

7. Serve fruit skewers with yogurt sauce as dip.

Smoked Seafood Ceviche

Preparation time: 20 minutes

Cooking time: 1 hour

Cooking method: Smoking

Makes: 8 servings

Temperature: 180°F, 325°F

Pellets: Mesquite

Ingredients:

- 2 lbs shrimp, peeled, deveined
- 2 lbs sea scallops, shucked
- 2 tbsp canola oil
- Juice of 2 oranges
- Juice of 2 lemons

- Juice of 2 limes
- Zest of 2 limes, grated
- 2 tsp garlic powder
- 1 tsp ground black pepper
- 1 red onion, diced
- 1/8 tsp red pepper flakes or to taste
- 4 tsp salt or to taste
- 2 avocados, peeled, pitted, diced
- A handful fresh cilantro, finely chopped
- Corn chips to serve

Directions:

1. Place scallops and shrimp in a bowl. Drizzle canola oil over it and toss well.
2. Operate the grill following the instructions of the manufacturer and light up the pellets. Set the grill on 'Smoke' option. Leave the lid open and let it operate for 10 minutes.
3. Set the temperature at 180°F and preheat the grill for 15 minutes. Close the lid while preheating.
4. Place the shrimp and scallops on the grill. Close the lid and let it smoke for 45 minutes.
5. Combine orange juice, lemon juice, lime juice, lime zest, garlic powder, pepper, red pepper flakes, onion and cilantro in a mixing bowl.
6. When the timer goes off, raise the temperature of the grill to 325°F and set the timer for 5 minutes.
7. Once cooked, remove scallops and shrimp from the grill and let it cool completely.
8. Cut them into two halves, widthwise. Add the seafood into the mixing bowl and toss well.
9. Cover and chill for three–four hours for the flavors to meld.
10. Serve ceviche with corn chips.

Baked Bacon Caramel Popcorn

Preparation time: 40 minutes

Cooking time: 30 minutes

Cooking method: Grilling

Makes: 12 servings

Temperature: 350°F, 225°F

Pellets: Mesquite

Ingredients:

- 2 lbs bacon
- 4 sticks unsalted butter
- 2 cups popcorn kernels
- 4 cups packed brown sugar
- 2 tsp baking soda

- ½ cup Kentucky bourbon
- 4 tsp vanilla extract
- 1 tsp salt

Directions:

1. Operate the grill following the instructions of the manufacturer and light up the pellets. Set the grill on 'Grill' option. Set the temperature at 350°F and preheat the grill for 15 minutes. Close the lid while preheating.

2. Place bacon strips on the grill grate and let it cook until slightly brown and the fat is released.

3. Take out the bacon strips from the grill and place it on your cutting board. When cool enough to handle, cut into ½ inch pieces. Now lower the temperature of the grill to 225°F and let the grill cool to this temperature.

4. Meanwhile, make popcorn in the popcorn maker as you normally do.

5. Transfer the popcorn into a large bowl. Add bacon and toss well.

6. Place a heavy bottomed saucepan over medium-high flame on your stovetop.

7. Add butter, salt and brown sugar and stir occasionally until the mixture is amber colored. Turn off the heat.

8. Carefully pour bourbon and vanilla. Add baking powder and whisk well.

9. Drizzle caramel sauce over popcorn and bacon and toss well.

10. Transfer the popcorn on a baking sheet. Use two baking sheets if required.

11. If the temperature of the grill has come down to 225°F, place the baking sheet in the oven. Cook for 15–20 minutes. Keep a watch over the popcorn. The caramel can burn so you need to watch it over.

12. Take out the baking sheet from the grill and let it cool for some time before serving.

Buffalo Chicken Dip

Preparation time: 10 minutes

Cooking time: 30 minutes

Cooking method: Grilling

Makes: 12 servings

Temperature: 350°F

Pellets: Mesquite

Ingredients:

- 16 oz cream cheese, softened
- 1 cup mayonnaise
- 2 tsp kosher salt

- 4 cups cooked, shredded chicken
- 1 cup sour cream
- 4 tbsp dry ranch dressing
- 1 cup Frank's red hot sauce
- 2 cups shredded cheddar cheese
- 1 cup blue cheese
- 2 cups shredded mozzarella cheese
- 8 strips bacon, cooked, crumbled

To serve: Use any

- Chips
- Crackers
- Crostini
- Vegetable sticks

Directions:

1. Operate the grill following the instructions of the manufacturer and light up the pellets. Set the grill on 'Grill' option. Set the temperature at 350°F and preheat the grill for 15 minutes. Close the lid while preheating.

2. Place cream cheese, mayonnaise, salt, sour cream, ranch seasoning and hot sauce in a mixing bowl.

3. Beat with an electric hand mixer until smooth and creamy.

4. Add cheddar cheese, chicken and mozzarella cheese and stir.

5. Spoon the mixture into a heatproof dish. Scatter blue cheese and bacon on top.

6. Now place the heatproof dish on the grill grate. Close the lid and cook until golden brown on top.

7. Serve with any of the suggested serving options.

Grilled Sweet Cajun Wings

Preparation time: 15 minutes

Cooking time: 30 minutes

Cooking method: Grilling

Makes: 8 servings

Temperature: 350°F

Pellets: Mesquite

Ingredients:

- Cajun dry rub, as required
- 4 lbs chicken wings

Directions:

1. Operate the grill following the instructions of the manufacturer and light up the pellets. Set the grill on 'Grill' option. Set the temperature at 350°F and preheat the grill for 15 minutes. Close the lid while preheating.

2. Sprinkle Cajun dry rub over the chicken wings and place them on the grill. Close the grill and grill for 30 minutes. When the wings are ready, the internal temperature of the meat in the center should show around 165°F.

3. Serve hot.

Ultimate Loaded Nachos

Preparation time: 15 minutes

Cooking time: 25 minutes

Cooking method: Grilling

Makes: 8 servings

Temperature: 375°F

Pellets: Hickory

Ingredients:

- 2 bags tortilla chips
- 2 cups cooked, shredded chicken breast
- 2 lbs kielbasa sausage, cooked, sliced
- 2 lbs tri-tip, cooked, cubed
- 1 cup fresh salsa
- ½ cup sliced scallions
- 3 cups shredded cheddar cheese
- 1 cup guacamole
- 2 small jars jalapeños, sliced
- 1 cup sour cream
- ½ cup chopped cilantro
- ½ cup sliced black olives

Directions:

1. Operate the grill following the instructions of the manufacturer and light up the pellets. Set the grill on 'Grill' option. Set the temperature at 375°F and preheat the grill for 15 minutes. Close the lid while preheating.

2. Place the tortilla chips on the baking sheet. Drizzle salsa over the chips. Place kielbasa sausage over the chips. Scatter chicken and tri-tip over the sausage.

3. Scatter scallions, olives and jalapeños all over the meat layer. Sprinkle cheese on top.

4. Place the baking sheet on the grill and close the lid. Cook until the cheese melts and the nachos are well heated.

Chapter 9:
Vegetarian Recipes

Chili Cheese Quesadillas

Preparation time: 15 minutes

Cooking time: 10 minutes

Cooking method: Grilling

Makes: 2–3 servings

Temperature: 350°F

Pellets: Apple or cherry

Ingredients:

- 4 oz cheddar cheese, chopped

- 2 tomatoes, peeled, deseeded, diced

- 2 small cloves garlic, peeled, minced

- A handful fresh cilantro, chopped

- 1 red chili, deseeded, finely chopped

- 1 shallot, finely chopped

- A handful pine nuts, toasted

- 6 flour tortillas (6 inches each)

Directions:

1. Operate the grill following the instructions of the manufacturer and light up the pellets. Select 'Grill' option. Set the temperature at 350°F and close the lid to preheat the grill.

2. Grease the grill grate.

3. Combine tomatoes, garlic, cilantro, red chili, shallot and pine nuts in a bowl.

4. Scatter the tomato mixture on one half of the tortillas. Divide the cheese among the tortillas and scatter it over the tomato mixture.

5. Fold the other half of the tortilla over the filling.

6. Place the quesadillas on the grill. Press the quesadillas slightly. When it is grilled to the desired doneness, flip sides and grill the other side as well.

7. Serve hot.

Green Bean Casserole

Preparation time: 5 minutes

Cooking time: 25 minutes

Cooking method: Grilling

Makes: 10–12 servings

Temperature: 375°F

Pellets: Pecan

Ingredients:

- 1 stick butter
- 1 cup sliced button mushrooms
- 4 cans cream of mushroom soup
- Ground black pepper to taste

- 2 cups grated sharp cheddar cheese
- 2 small onions, chopped
- 8 cans green beans, drained
- 2 tsp Lawry's seasoned salt
- 2 cans crispy fried onions

Directions:

1. Operate the grill following the instructions of the manufacturer and light up the pellets. Select the 'Grill' option. Set the temperature at 375°F and close the lid to preheat the grill.

2. Place a cast iron skillet on the grill. Add butter. Once butter melts, add onion and mushrooms and sauté until soft.

3. Stir in green beans and cream of mushroom soup. Add pepper and Lawry's seasoned salt and stir. Sprinkle cheddar cheese and fried onion on top.

4. Place on the grill. Close the lid and cook for 25 minutes.

5. Cool for a few minutes and serve.

Roasted Carrot Salad with Smoked Pickled Beets

Preparation time: 30 minutes

Cooking time: 2 hours

Cooking method: Smoking

Makes: 3 servings

Temperature: 185 °F, 500 °F

Pellets: Cherry

Ingredients:

For salad:

- 1 lb beets
- 3 medium carrots, cut into ½ inch rounds
- ¼ cup chopped fresh parsley
- Salt to taste
- Pepper to taste
- ¼ cup crumbled feta cheese
- 1 ½ tsp olive oil, divided

For brine:

- ¼ tsp mustard seeds
- 1 bay leaf
- ¼ bunch dill leaves
- 1 cup white vinegar
- ½ cup sugar
- ¼ onion, sliced
- 1 tsp black peppercorns
- 2 cloves garlic, smashed
- ½ cup water

For dressing:

- 1 tsp fresh lemon juice
- ½ tsp Dijon mustard

- ½ tbsp finely chopped fresh mint
- Salt to taste
- ½ tsp ground cumin
- Pepper to taste
- 1 tsp sherry vinegar
- ¼ cup

Directions:

1. Place beets in a saucepan filled with water and cook until tender. Add salt to the water while boiling.

2. Drain off the water and cool the beets for a while. When cool enough to handle, peel the beets.

3. Operate the grill following the instructions of the manufacturer and light up the pellets. Set the grill on 'Smoke' option. Leave the lid open and let it operate for 10 minutes. Set the temperature at 185°F and close the lid to preheat the grill.

4. Smoke the beets on the grill for an hour.

5. Take out the beets and when cool enough to handle, cut into ½ inch pieces.

6. Place them in a heatproof bowl.

7. To make brine: Combine water, vinegar, sugar, onion, bay leaf, onion, peppercorns, mustard, garlic and dill in a saucepan.

8. Place the saucepan on the grill and cook until sugar dissolves completely and the brine comes to a boil.

9. Pour the brine over the beets. Keep a plate over the beets so that they remain immersed in the brine.

10. Place carrots in a saucepan filled with water and cook for only a minute. Add salt to the water while boiling.

11. Drain off the water and cool the carrots for a while.

12. To make dressing: Combine cumin, salt, pepper, vinegar, Dijon mustard, lemon juice and mint in a bowl.

13. Pour ¼ cup oil, whisking simultaneously. Cover and set aside for a while for the flavors to blend in. Raise the temperature of the grill to 500 °F and let it preheat.

14. Place carrot slices on a baking sheet. Brush ¾ tsp oil over the carrot slices.

15. Drain off the brine or use it in some other recipe. Brush ¾ tsp oil over the beets and place it on the baking sheet along with the carrots.

16. Place the baking sheet on the grill and grill for 15–20 minutes. Flip sides half way through baking.

17. Combine beets, carrots, cheese and parsley in a bowl. Pour dressing on top. Toss well and serve.

Smoked Mac & Cheese

Preparation time: 40 minutes

Cooking time: 1 hour

Cooking method: Smoking

Makes: 8 servings

Temperature: 180°F, 350°F

Pellets: Hickory

Ingredients:

- 5 cups half and half + extra if required
- 16 oz cream cheese, cut into small cubes
- 2 tsp dry mustard
- 32 oz elbow macaroni
- 3 cups shredded smoked mozzarella or gouda cheese
- 2 cups panko breadcrumbs
- 10 tbsp chilled butter + extra to grease the pan
- 2 tsp hot sauce or to taste
- 1-½ tsp ground black pepper
- 3 cups cheddar cheese
- 4 tbsp butter, melted
- Salt to taste

Directions:

1. Operate the grill following the instructions of the manufacturer and light up the pellets. Set the grill on 'Smoke' option. Leave the lid open and let it operate for 10 minutes. Set the temperature at 180°F and close the lid to preheat the grill.

2. Place eight tablespoons of chilled butter, hot sauce, black pepper, half and half, cream cheese and mustard in a large cast iron skillet.

3. Place the skillet on the grill. Set the timer for 30 minutes and smoke the sauce mixture. Stir occasionally. Once the timer goes off, remove the skillet from the grill.

4. Meanwhile, cook the pasta on your stovetop by following the directions on the package but drain the pasta a couple of minutes earlier than that mentioned on the package. Drain and add the pasta back into the pot. Add all the cheeses into the pot.

5. Raise the temperature of the grill to 350°F. Close the lid and let it preheat for 15 minutes.

6. Pour the sauce mixture into the pot of pasta and toss well.

7. Grease the cast iron skillet with two tablespoons of chilled butter. Spoon the macaroni mixture into the skillet.

8. Mix together breadcrumbs and melted butter in a bowl. Scatter this mixture over the macaroni.

9. Place the skillet on the grill and close the lid. Grill for 30–40 minutes or until brown on top.

10. Sprinkle paprika on top and serve.

Chapter 10:
Desserts

Bacon Sweet Potato Pie

Preparation time: 30 minutes

Cooking time: 1-½ hours

Cooking method: Grilling

Makes: 12–15 servings

Temperature: 350°F

Pellets: Apple or cherry or pecan

Ingredients:

- 2.6 lbs sweet potatoes, peeled, cubed
- 1-½ cups packed dark brown sugar
- ½ tsp ground nutmeg
- ½ tsp salt
- 2 cups chopped pecans, toasted
- 2 tbsp maple syrup
- 2-½ cups plain yogurt
- 1 tsp ground cinnamon
- 10 egg yolks
- 2 deep dish frozen pie shells (9 inches each)
- 8 strips bacon, cooked, diced
- Whipped topping to serve (optional)

Directions:

1. To make filling: Place a pot of water over your stove top and bring to a boil. Place a steamer basket in the pot and the sweet potatoes in the basket. Steam for 20 minutes or until soft.

2. Mash the sweet potatoes with a potato masher.

3. Operate the grill following the instructions of the manufacturer and light up the pellets. Set the grill on the 'Grill' option. Set the temperature at 350°F and preheat the grill for 15 minutes. Close the lid while preheating.

4. Transfer the sweet potatoes into the mixing bowl of the stand mixer. Beat the sweet potatoes using the paddle attachment.

5. Beat in brown sugar, yogurt, yolks, salt and spices. Once combined, divide the filling among the pie crusts.

6. Place the pie crusts on a large baking sheet. Scatter pecans and bacon on top. Drizzle a tbsp of maple syrup on each pie.

7. Place the baking sheet on the grill and bake for 45–60 minutes or until set and the temperature of the custard is 165°F–180°F.

8. Cool completely. Cut into wedges and serve.

Mango Macadamia Crisp

Preparation time: 15–20 minutes

Cooking time: 1 hour

Cooking method: Grilling

Makes: 4 servings

Temperature: 350°F

Pellets: Apple or cherry

Ingredients:

- 2-½ cups thinly sliced fresh ripe mango
- 1 tbsp all-purpose flour
- 1 tbsp candied ginger, minced
- 2 tbsp brown sugar or to taste
- Zest of ½ lemon, grated
- Juice of a lemon

For the topping:

- 2 tbsp cold butter, chopped
- ¼ cup macadamia nuts, coarsely chopped
- 2 tbsp all-purpose flour
- ¼ cup shredded sweetened coconut
- ¼ cup shortbread or butter cookies, crushed
- A pinch salt
- 2 tbsp firmly packed brown sugar
- ½ tsp ground cinnamon
- Whipped cream or vanilla ice cream to serve (optional)

Directions:

1. Combine brown sugar, candied ginger, lemon juice and lemon zest in a glass bowl and toss well. Add flour and mix well. Transfer the mixture into a cast-iron skillet and set aside.

2. Place butter, macadamia nuts, flour, coconut, shortbread, salt, brown sugar and cinnamon in the food processor bowl and give short pulses until the mixture is coarse. The butter should become smaller in size. Sprinkle this mixture over the mangoes.

3. Operate the grill following the instructions of the manufacturer and light up the pellets. Set the grill on 'Grill' option. Set the temperature at 350°F and preheat the grill for 15 minutes. Close the lid while preheating.

4. Place the skillet on the grill. Close the lid and set the timer for 40–60 minutes or until brown on top.

5. Remove from the grill and cool for a while. Serve warm, as it is, or with ice cream.

Grilled Apple Crisp

Preparation time: 15 minutes

Cooking time: 30 minutes

Cooking method: Grilling

Makes: 12 servings

Temperature: 350°F

Pellets: Apple

Ingredients:

- 6 apples, cored, halved
- 1 cup granola
- 2 tbsp maple syrup
- 1 stick butter

- 2 handfuls craisins
- Juice of a lemon
- 2 tbsp pumpkin pie spice or apple pie spice
- 3 heaping tbsp brown sugar
- ¼ cup chopped pecans or any other nuts of your choice

Directions:

1. Operate the grill following the instructions of the manufacturer and light up the pellets. Set the grill on 'Grill' option. Set the temperature at 350°F and preheat the grill for 15 minutes. Close the lid while preheating.

2. Place the apple halves on a baking sheet or baking pan after cutting off a thin slice from the bottom of the apple halves so that they can stand on the baking sheet without wobbling. Remove a little more of the apple flesh near the cored area, to create a cavity. Brush lemon juice on the cut part of the apples.

3. Combine granola, brown sugar, spices and maple syrup in a bowl.

4. Fill the apples with this mixture and make a mound of it as well.

5. Place the baking sheet on the grill and grill for about 30 minutes or until golden brown on top and the apples are cooked.

6. Serve as it is or with ice cream.

Chapter 11:

Tips and Tricks

Investing in a wood pellet smoker grill is a wonderful idea but it is a significant investment, so you need to make the most of it. To do this, start using the different tips and suggestions discussed in this section. Apart from this, another obvious tip you need to remember while using this appliance is to keep it clean. The buildup of food waste and grime reduces the grill's ability to smoke and cook food properly. By using the different tips discussed in the section, you can up your grilling game within no time. Don't stifle your creativity, experiment with the different recipes given in this book, and cook delicious food!

Understand the Ingredients

Before you start cooking, it is important to understand what you want to cook. Every type of meat needs to be treated differently and every cut differs. By understanding the composition of the meat—whether it has a bone, it's fat content, muscle, and cartilage— you can cook it to perfection. Apart from this, you need to consider the texture of the cut and whether it is dark or white meat. Maybe you want to smoke vegetables or even cheese. Before you start smoking any ingredient in the wood pellet smoker grill, think about what you want to do with it. The great news is, all the recipes you need to make the most of your wood pellet smoker grill are included in this book.

Try Reverse Searing

Reverse searing is one technique you need to use with a pellet grill. If you like the idea of a medium-rare finish on meats with a perfectly seared edge and a smoky flavor, reverse sear the meats. Reverse searing essentially refers to a process where the ingredients are baked in the oven and then seared on a pan. It offers more control over the internal temperature of the meat while keeping it tender with a perfectly seared crust. Start by cooking the meat on an upper rack until it is almost cooked or has reached the internal temperature of 125° (for medium-rare beef). After this, place it on the lower grill and crank up the heat for the perfect finish.

Use It Like an Oven

A straightforward and effective trick is to use a pellet grill like an oven. If a recipe calls for baking or roasting in an oven, transfer it to the pellet smoker. The cooking time and temperature stay the same. You will certainly change your mind once you experiment with the various dessert recipes given in this book.

Smoke Cold Meats

Did you know that smoke loves cold meats? The colder the meat, the greater the chance of the smoke condensing onto its surface. Instead of allowing the meat to come up to room temperature, place it in the pellet smoker straight out of the fridge after massaging it with some dry rub or marinade of your choice. Smoking the meat overnight creates a more pronounced smoky flavor.

Conclusion

Thank you one again for choosing this book. I hope you enjoyed the recipes and are raring to start your grill.

This book has many easy and delicious wood pellet smoker grill recipes. These recipes are divided into different categories for your convenience. Whether you wish to grill or smoke beef, seafood, poultry, or any other meats including appetizers, sides, and even desserts, there's plenty to choose from. Apart from all this, it also includes several recipes to make delicious homemade marinades, sauces, rubs, and glazes. All these recipes are incredibly simple to understand and easy to cook. As long as you gather the required ingredients and follow the recipe, you can grill or smoke meats and other ingredients to perfection!

While using the wood pellet smoker grill, don't forget to use the various tips and tricks to enhance the cooking results. All the information you need to make the most of your wood pellet smoker grill is provided within this book. Now, all that's left for you to do is select a recipe that you want to cook, gather the necessary ingredients, and get cooking.

Thank you and all the best!

References

Braby, E. (2020, May 10). 9 Pellet Grill Tips and Tricks: Get The Most Out of Your Smoker. Food Fire Friends website: https://www.foodfirefriends.com/pellet-grill-tips/

How Do Pellet Grills Work? Pellet Grills 101 | Pit Boss Grills. (n.d.). pitboss-grills.com website: Https://pitboss-grills.com/pellet-grills-101-how-they-work

Why Should I Try a Pellet Grill, What is it? (2016, August 5). Grilla Grills website: Https://grillagrills.com/why-should-i-try/#:~:text=Pellet%20Grills%20Offer%20a%20Quick%20Heat%20Up&text=Pellet%20grills%20allow%20busy%20people,flavor%20of%20cooking%20over%20wood.

BOOK 2

Wood Pellet Recipe Book

How to Grill Everything: The Complete Guide With Simple Recipes for Your BBQ

Adam Greenwood

Introduction

Are you bored and tired of spending hours together in front of your regular conventional grill only to have the food unevenly cooked? Does your grilled food taste more like coal than the meat flavor? Are you looking for an easier way to get the desired delicious and smoky flavor into your meats and other foods? If yes, then it is time to upgrade your conventional grill and try out the wood pellet smoker and grill.

This book is perfect for new wood pellet grill owners or those who want to trade their old grilling methods for a new one. In the course of this book, you will learn about the structure and components of a wood pellet smoker grill, the reasons why cooking with it is amazing, and a few simple tips on how to use it. You will also learn about flavorful food-grade wood pellets to perfectly complement everyday ingredients to obtain incredible results. By using the various cooking tips and tricks discussed in this book, you can grill meats like a professional chef.

This book has loads of wood pellet smoker grill recipes using different meats as well as veggies. All these recipes are incredibly easy to follow, are divided into different categories for your convenience—and they include recipes for delicious rubs, marinades sauces, and glazes. These simple and delicious recipes yield incredible results.

Now you can impress your friends and family with a perfectly cooked and smoked piece of meat at the next barbecue party. The best part is you could do all this without any of the hassles usually associated with grilling and smoking. All you have to do is make sure that your pantry is stocked with the required ingredients, choose a recipe that you fancy, make some kick-ass glaze, sauce or marinade and get started! Soon you will be the BBQ expert, as your friends and family members seek invites to your coveted grills and BBQ nights.

If you are ready to learn more about this and get started, read on. Thank you for choosing this book, I hope you enjoy it.

Chapter 1:

What is a Wood Pellet Smoker Grill

Pellet grills are versatile outdoor cookers that efficiently combine the elements of different cooking appliances, such as smoker, oven, and gas or charcoal grills. As the name suggests, pellet grills use wood pellets as the fuel source. Ingredients can be cooked via direct or indirect heat, depending on the placement of the rack Understanding the inner workings, structure, and components of the wood pellet smoker grill helps make the most of its features. Even if it seems a little overwhelming initially, it is quite straightforward.

Structure of a Wood Pellet Smoker Grill

A wood pellet smoker grill consists of a hopper, firepot, auger, hot rod, heat deflector, induction fan, resistance temperature detector, flame zone pan, and grease bucket.

The part of the appliance where the wood pellets are filled is known as the hopper. The firepot is the area directly under the grill where the fire is lit. The auger helps to transport the wood pellets from the hopper to the firepot. The hot rod or the igniter element ignites the flame to start a fire once the wood pellets are in the firepot.

The induction fan present in this appliance helps to stoke the flames and evenly distribute the heat. These elements turn the regular grill and smoker into an appliance with functionalities similar to an oven. The temperature of the grill and smoker is measured by the resistance temperature detector.

There exists a barrier between the flames in the firepot and the grill known as the heat deflector. It helps redirect the heat to promote even cooking while reducing the risk of burning or charring. You can use the flame zone pan coupled with griddle accessories and a searing grate to grill foods at high temperatures without using a barrier to separate the two. Using a grease bucket prevents any fats or oils from dripping into the flames.

Why Choose This?

Wood pellet smoker grills are user-friendly so, irrespective whether you are a newbie or a pro, grilling and smoking meats is easy. You don't have to worry about any sudden flare-ups so ensuring an even cook on the meats is almost always guaranteed. It also reduces the risk of charring meat due to exposure to uneven temperatures.

This is an incredible appliance with multiple uses. You can grill and smoke a variety of meats, seafood, and poultry. You can also use it instead of an oven. You can cook sides, appetizers, and even desserts on a wood pellet grill. By merely changing the placement of the ingredients between the top and lower racks and varying the temperature, you can use it to cook a variety of ingredients.

In the previous section, you were introduced to the basic structure and components of a typical wood pellet smoker grill. That's about it. There is no learning curve involved here. When in doubt, follow the instructions given in the recipes shared in the subsequent chapters of this book, and cook like a pro!

Wood pellet smoker grills are cost- and fuel-efficient. They need around a pound of wood pellets per hour of cooking time. Another benefit of this incredible appliance is that you don't have to worry about transferring or lugging any heavy propane tanks. So, they are safer and easier to use.

If you love the idea of grilled and smoked foods, but don't have the time or patience for it, this is the perfect appliance for you. For instance, to get the best results, you need to smoke meat overnight. Rub the meat with a dry rub or a marinade, set the temperature on the wood pellet smoker grill, and leave it overnight! Yes, it is as simple as that!

Another advantage of the wood pellet smoker grill is that the external temperature does not affect the cooking procedure. As long as the internal temperature of the grill is maintained, you have nothing to worry about.

How to Use a Wood Pellet Smoker Grill

Before you start using the wood pellet smoker grill, ensure that you give it a dry run. It helps to burn any traces of contaminants, chemicals, and other pollutants that might have been leftover from the manufacturing process. The burn-in procedure is quite simple. Simply fill the hopper and half the firepot with wood pallets and plug in the appliance. Set the temperature between 350–450°F and the flames will last for an hour. Don't forget to go through the instruction manual to check the ideal temperature for the dry run.

To improve the overall results obtained from the wood pellet grill, season the grill before you start cooking. The simplest way to season the grill is by cooking bacon at 350°F for about an hour.

If you want your food to be infused only with clean smoke whenever you cook, ensure that you clean this appliance. It hardly takes a couple of minutes to clean the smoker grill. Clean the grill grates using a wire brush while they're still hot and then wipe them with a warm cloth or paper towel. When the fire pot is completely cool, remove the drip pan and use a degreaser to clean it thoroughly. Always remove all traces of ash from the body of the grill and the firepot. If the ash starts piling up, the overall efficiency of the grill reduces. Ensure that there are no traces of old grease after you use the wood pellet smoker grill.

About Food-Grade Wood Pellets

Whenever you purchase wood pellets for the smoker grill, ensure that you use food-grade barbecue wood pellets. These specific pellets do not contain any harmful chemicals and foreign pollutants. They also don't have any additives except for vegetable oils which reduce the ash that's left over after grilling and smoking. Food-grade wood chips are usually cylindrical with a 1/4-inch diameter.

Food-grade wood pellets usually come in a combination of flavors that are either made from oak or alder. Each type of wood has a specific flavor that pairs well with certain types of meats. The percentage of the flavor varies from one manufacturer to another.

To improve the overall taste and smoke intensity of the resultant product, pair wood pallets with specific foods. For instance, apple has a strong aroma that smells and pairs incredibly well with all types of game meats, pork, poultry, and lamb. Alder pairs well with fatty fish such as salmon, pork poultry, beef, and lamb because of its mild and sweet taste and aroma. Cherry wood has a slightly sweet flavor that lends a rosy hue to the meats. Cherry wood chips are the perfect match for game meat, beef, poultry, and pork. The tangy, sweet, and mild flavor of maple pairs well with poultry, beef, and pork. Mesquite's tangy and spicy flavor is well-suited for all types of meats except fish. One of the most commonly used wood pellets is hickory. It's bacon-like aroma and taste bonds well with all types of meats. Beef, pork, and poultry can be paired with the spicy and nutty flavor of pecan wood chips.

Before you purchase any wood pellets, read through the list of ingredients to determine the percentage of flavor. Experiment with all these combinations to find something you love and enjoy. Allow your creativity and imagination to run wild as you experiment with different flavored wood pellets and meats.

Chapter 2:
Recipes for Rubs, Marinades, Sauces and Glaze

BBQ Rub Recipes

Honey Sriracha Marinade

Makes: About 1/3 cup

Ingredients:

- 3 tbsp honey
- 2 tsp sriracha chili sauce
- 1/8 tsp salt or to taste
- 2 tbsp soy sauce or tamari
- 2 tsp rice vinegar or apple cider vinegar
- 2 cloves garlic, peeled, minced

Directions:

1. Whisk together honey, sriracha chili sauce, salt, soy sauce, garlic and rice vinegar in a bowl.

2. To use: Marinate the chicken in this mixture for 30 minutes before grilling.

Buffalo Marinade

Makes: About 1-1/8 cups

Ingredients:

- ½ cup Frank's hot wings sauce or Frank's original hot sauce
- 2 tbsp lime juice
- 2 tsp chili powder
- 1 tsp ground cumin
- 1 tsp onion powder
- 2 tsp garlic powder
- 2 tsp salt
- 2 tsp smoked paprika
- ½ tsp ground black pepper
- 4 tbsp honey
- 4 tbsp olive oil

Directions:

1. Combine hot wings sauce, lime juice, honey salt and all the spices in a bowl. Add olive oil and stir until well combined.

2. How to use: Add chicken into the marinade and stir until well coated. Cover the bowl and place in the refrigerator for two–eight hours.

3. Remove from the refrigerator an hour before grilling.

Sauce Recipes

Simple Honey Mustard Sauce

Makes: About 2-¼ cups

Ingredients:

- 2/3 cup honey
- 1-½ cups Dijon mustard

Directions:

1. Whisk together honey and Dijon mustard in a bowl.

2. Cover and chill until use. It can last for two weeks.

3. This sauce can be used as a dip or as a glaze as well.

Kansas City-Style BBQ Sauce

Makes: 4 cups

Ingredients:

- 3 cups ketchup
- 1 cup water
- 2 tbsp Worcestershire sauce
- 2 tsp kosher salt
- 1 tsp onion powder
- 1 tsp paprika
- ¾ cups packed brown sugar
- ½ cup apple cider vinegar

- 4 tbsp molasses
- 1 tsp garlic powder
- ½ tsp ground mustard

Directions:

1. Combine ketchup, water, Worcestershire sauce, salt, brown sugar, paprika, vinegar, molasses, garlic powder and mustard in a saucepan.

2. Place the saucepan over medium flame. When the mixture comes to a boil, lower the flame and cook until thick, stir often. Turn off the heat.

White Barbecue Sauce

Makes: About 1-1/3 cups

Ingredients:

- 1 cup mayonnaise
- Juice of a lemon
- 1 tsp Dijon mustard

- Freshly ground black pepper
- 4 tbsp apple cider vinegar
- 2 tbsp horseradish
- Cayenne pepper to taste
- Salt to taste

Directions:

1. Whisk together mayonnaise, lemon juice, Dijon mustard, pepper, apple cider vinegar, horseradish, cayenne pepper and salt in a bowl.

Spicy Honey Mustard Barbecue Sauce

Makes: About 1 cup

Ingredients:

- 1-½ cups yellow mustard
- 2 tsp garlic powder
- 2 tbsp Worcestershire sauce

- 2 pickled jalapeño peppers, minced
- 2 tbsp ketchup
- 6 tbsp honey or more to taste
- tsp freshly ground pepper
- 12 tbsp cider vinegar
- 4 tbsp Frank's red hot sauce or any other hot sauce

Directions:

1. Whisk together mustard, garlic powder, Worcestershire sauce, jalapeño peppers, ketchup, pepper, cider vinegar, hot sauce and honey in a saucepan.

2. Place the saucepan over medium flame. Stir often until the mixture begins to simmer.

3. Lower the flame and cook for about 12–15 minutes or until the sauce is thickened to the desired consistency.

4. Turn off the heat and pour into an airtight container. Let it cool completely. Cover the container and chill until further use.

Horseradish Sauce

Makes: 4 cups

Ingredients:

- ½ cup prepared horseradish in vinegar
- 1 cup milk
- 2 tsp kosher salt
- 2 cups sour cream
- ½ cup mayonnaise
- Zest of 2 lemons, grated

Directions:

1. Combine horseradish, milk, salt, sour cream, sour cream, mayonnaise and lemon in a bowl.
2. Cover and chill for 24–26 hours.
3. Serve.

BBQ Rum Sauce

Makes: About 2 cups

Ingredients:

- 1 can (8 oz) tomato sauce
- 1 small onion, chopped
- 2 tbsp dark rum
- 1 clove garlic, peeled minced
- ½ tbsp Worcestershire sauce
- ½ tbsp paprika
- ½ can (from an 8 oz can) green chilies
- ¼ cup brown sugar
- 1 tbsp vinegar

- ½ tbsp molasses
- ½ tbsp olive oil

Directions:

1. Pour olive oil into a saucepan and heat over medium flame.
2. Once oil is heated, add onion and garlic and cook until onion turns translucent.
3. Stir in tomato sauce, Worcestershire sauce, paprika, chilies, brown sugar, vinegar and molasses.
4. Stir frequently until brown sugar dissolves completely. When the mixture begins to simmer, turn off the heat.
5. Stir in the rum. Blend the mixture until smooth.
6. The sauce is ready to serve.

South Carolina Mustard Barbecue Sauce

Makes: About ¼ cup

Ingredients:

- 6 tbsp yellow mustard
- ½ tbsp Worcestershire sauce
- ½ tbsp ketchup
- ¼ tsp freshly ground pepper
- 3 tbsp cider vinegar
- ½ tbsp Frank's red hot sauce or any other hot sauce
- 2–3 tbsp packed brown sugar

Directions:

1. Whisk together mustard, Worcestershire sauce, ketchup, pepper, cider vinegar, hot sauce and brown sugar in a saucepan.
2. Place the saucepan over medium flame. Stir often until the mixture begins to simmer.
3. Lower the flame and cook for about 12–15 minutes or until the sauce is one-third

of its original quantity.

4. Turn off the heat and pour into an airtight container. Let it cool completely. Cover the container and chill until further use.

Southwestern Barbecue Sauce

Makes: About 3-½ cups

Ingredients:

- 2 cups ketchup
- ½ cup lime juice
- 2 tbsp chili powder
- 4 tsp ground cumin
- 1 cup brown sugar
- ½ cup white vinegar
- 2 tsp chipotle chili powder
- 1 tsp salt

Directions:

1. Combine ketchup, lime juice, brown sugar, all the spices and salt in a saucepan.

2. Place the saucepan over medium flame. Stir often until the mixture begins to simmer.

3. Lower the flame and cook for about 12–15 minutes or until the sauce is thickened to the desired consistency.

4. Turn off the heat and pour into an airtight container. Let it cool completely. Cover the container and chill until further use. Use it within two weeks.

Mumbo Sauce

Makes: About 4-½ cups

Ingredients:

- 2 cups ketchup
- ½ cup granulated sugar
- ½ cup water or pineapple juice or apricot nectar
- 1 tsp sweet mild paprika
- Salt to taste
- ½ cups golden syrup or light corn syrup
- 2/3 cup white vinegar
- 4 tbsp soy sauce
- 1 tsp hot sauce or more to taste

Directions:

1. Combine ketchup, sugar, water, paprika, salt, syrup, white vinegar, soy sauce and hot sauce in a saucepan.

2. Place the saucepan over medium flame. Stir often until the mixture begins to simmer.

3. Lower the flame and cook for about 12–15 minutes or until the sauce is thickened to the desired consistency.

4. Turn off the heat and pour into an airtight container. Let it cool completely. Cover the container and chill until use. Use it within two weeks.

5. You can use this sauce as a glaze, as well.

Sweet Finishing Sauce for Brisket

Makes: About 1 cup

Ingredients:

- 1 can tomato paste
- 2 tbsp brown sugar
- ½ tbsp white vinegar
- 1/8 tsp black pepper
- 6 tbsp water
- ½ tsp ground cinnamon
- ¼ tsp salt

Directions:

1. Combine tomato paste, brown sugar, white vinegar, pepper, water, cinnamon and salt in a saucepan.

2. Place the saucepan over medium flame. Stir often until the mixture begins to simmer.

3. Add more water if required. Turn off the heat. Cool completely and transfer into an airtight container. Chill until use. It can last for a week.

4. Serve alongside grilled brisket. This sauce is not meant to be used while grilling.

Creamy Roasted Red Pepper Sauce

Makes: About 2 cups

Ingredients:

- 2 large red bell peppers
- 4–6 shallots, peeled
- 4 tbsp heavy whipping cream
- 2 tbsp butter

- Cayenne pepper to taste
- 2 tbsp tomato paste
- Salt to taste
- 1 cup vegetable broth
- Pepper to taste

Directions:

1. Set up your oven to broil mode and broil the bell peppers until charred all over. Turn often. You can also roast it directly on an open flame on your stove top.

2. Let it cool for a while on your countertop. Remove the peel, seeds and membranes from the bell peppers and chop into smaller pieces.

3. Add butter into a saucepan and melt over medium-low flame. Add shallots and cook for a minute.

4. Stir in roasted bell peppers and broth and bring to a boil. Let it cook for a couple of minutes. Turn off the heat.

5. Cool for a few minutes and blend the mixture until smooth. Add cayenne pepper and blend until well combined.

6. Place a strainer over a saucepan. Pour the blended mixture into the strainer and strain the mixture.

7. Add tomato paste and heavy whipping cream into the saucepan. Heat the mixture over low flame until nice and hot.

8. Pour into a bowl. Garnish with cilantro sprigs, if desired, and serve.

Citrus Cranberry Sauce

Makes: About 1 cup

Ingredients:

- 1 naval orange, peeled, separate into segments, cut into pieces
- ½ lb fresh or frozen cranberries
- ¼ cup water

- ½ lemon
- 2 tbsp sugar

Directions:

1. Grate some of the peel of orange and lemon. Measure out one-half teaspoon of each and place in a bowl. Use the lemon in some other recipe.

2. Place cranberries, water and sugar in a saucepan. Heat over medium-high flame. Stir often until sugar dissolves completely.

3. Slowly the cranberries will start bubbling and the sauce will start getting thick. Cook for five–six minutes. Turn off the heat.

4. Add orange zest, lemon zest and orange segments and stir. Let it cool completely.

5. Transfer into an airtight container and refrigerate for at least three hours before using.

Lemony Tahini Sauce

Makes: About 1 cup

Ingredients:

- ½ cup tahini paste
- 2 tbsp fresh lemon juice
- ¾ tsp kosher salt
- ¼ tsp lemon zest
- ½ tsp minced garlic
- ½ cup water
- A pinch Aleppo chili pepper + extra to serve

Directions:

1. Combine tahini, garlic, lemon juice and about ¼ cup water in a bowl. Whisk until smooth. Add remaining water, a little at a time and whisk well each time. Add water until you get the desired consistency.

2. Stir in Aleppo pepper, lemon juice, salt and lemon zest. Taste and add more salt

and lemon juice if required. Add more Aleppo pepper if you like it spicy.

3. Transfer into an airtight container and chill until use. It can last for five days.

4. Sprinkle some Aleppo pepper on top and serve.

Chimichurri Sauce

Makes: About ¾ cup

Ingredients:

- 1 cup minced, packed flat-leaf parsley
- ½ cup extra-virgin olive oil
- 2-½ tbsp plum vinegar
- ½ tbsp kosher salt
- 2–3 chili peppers
- 2 tbsp minced fresh oregano
- 2–3 cloves garlic, peeled, minced
- ½ Serrano chili pepper or use more if you like it hot
- Freshly ground pepper to taste

Directions:

1. Set up your oven to broil mode and broil the Serrano chili pepper until charred all over and blackish. Turn often. You can also roast it directly on an open flame

on your stove top.

2. Place Serrano pepper into a blender. Also add oil, vinegar, salt, chili peppers, oregano, garlic, and pepper and blend until smooth.

3. Pour into a bowl. Cover and chill for two–three hours for the flavors to meld. It can last for a week.

Herb and Garlic Yogurt Sauce

Makes: About ½ cup

Ingredients:

- 1 Serrano chili
- ½ cup chopped cilantro leaves and tender stems or mint or dill or any other herbs of your choice
- ½ tbsp extra-virgin olive oil
- Salt to taste
- 1 clove garlic, peeled
- ¼ cup full-fat Greek yogurt
- ½ tsp honey
- 2 tbsp water

Directions:

1. Place chili, cilantro, oil, salt, garlic, yogurt, honey, and water in a blender and blend until smooth.

2. Pour into a bowl. Cover and chill until use. Use within three days.

Pineapple Sauce & Glaze

Makes: About 2/3 cup

Ingredients:

- ½ cup packed brown sugar
- 1/8 tsp salt
- 1 tbsp lemon juice
- ½ tbsp cornstarch
- ½ can (from an 8.5 oz can) crushed pineapple with syrup
- ½ tbsp mustard

Directions:

1. Combine brown sugar, salt, lemon juice, pineapple, and mustard in a saucepan.

2. Place the saucepan over medium flame and keep stirring until the brown sugar dissolves completely.

3. Continue cooking until the consistency you desire is achieved.

4. This sauce is mostly used for ham. This sauce can also be used as glaze, as well.

Gochujang Barbecue Sauce

Makes: About 1 1/8 cups

Ingredients:

- 1/3 cup apple cider vinegar
- 3 tbsp gochujang (Korean hot chili paste)
- ¼ cup dark brown sugar
- 2 tbsp adobo sauce (from the can of chipotle chilies in adobo sauce)

Directions:

1. Combine apple cider vinegar, gochujang, brown sugar and adobo sauce in a bowl. This sauce is generally used to grill pork ribs and serve as a dip along with it as well.

Glaze Recipes

Spicy Maple Glaze

Makes: About 1/3 cup

Ingredients:

- ¼ cup maple syrup
- 2 small cloves garlic, peeled, minced
- ½ tbsp Dijon mustard
- ½ tbsp sriracha sauce
- ½ tbsp soy sauce
- ½ cup water

Directions:

1. Combine maple syrup, garlic, Dijon mustard, sriracha sauce, soy sauce and water in a saucepan.

2. Place the saucepan over medium flame. Stir often until the mixture begins to simmer.

3. Lower the flame and cook for about 12–15 minutes or until the sauce is thickened to the desired consistency.

4. Turn off the heat and pour into an airtight container. Let it cool completely. Cover the container and chill until further use. Use it within two weeks.

Citrus Glaze

Makes: 1 cup

Ingredients:

- ½ cup lemon marmalade
- 4 tbsp packed brown sugar
- 4 tbsp fresh orange juice

Directions:

1. Whisk together marmalade, brown sugar and orange juice in a bowl. Keep whisking until sugar dissolves completely.

2. Refrigerate until use. Use within two–three days.

Buffalo Glaze

Makes: About ¼ cup

Ingredients:

- 2 tbsp Frank's hot wings sauce or Frank's original hot sauce
- 1-½ tbsp lime juice
- ½ tsp chili powder
- ¼ tsp ground cumin
- ¼ tsp onion powder
- ½ tsp garlic powder
- ½ tsp salt
- ½ tsp smoked paprika
- 1/8 tsp ground black pepper
- 1 ½ tbsp honey

Directions:

1. Combine hot wings sauce, lime juice, honey, salt, and all the spices in a bowl.

Two Mustard Honey Glaze

Makes: About 4 cups

Ingredients:

- 2 cups honey
- 1 cup ground mustard
- Ground black pepper to taste
- 1 cup Dijon mustard
- Salt to taste

Directions:

1. Whisk together honey, ground mustard, salt, pepper and Dijon mustard in an airtight container.
2. Cover the container and chill. It can last for two weeks.

Currant Jelly Glaze

Makes: About 1-½ cups

Ingredients:

- ½ jar (from a 10 oz jar) red currant jelly
- ½ cup orange juice
- 1-½ tbsp spicy brown mustard
- ½ cup firmly packed brown sugar
- ¼ cup dry sherry

Directions:

1. Combine red currant jelly, orange juice, mustard, brown sugar and dry sherry in a saucepan.
2. Place the saucepan over medium flame and heat until the mixture is smooth. Make sure to keep stirring until smooth.

3. Turn off the heat. Pour into an airtight container. Cool completely. Cover the container and store at room temperature. It can last for two days.

4. This glaze is generally used on ham.

Honey Barbecue Glaze

Makes: 1 cup

Ingredients:

- ½ cup honey
- 2 tbsp ketchup
- 4 tsp Worcestershire sauce
- 1–2 tsp sriracha sauce
- 2 tbsp soy sauce
- 4 tsp Dijon mustard
- ½ tsp cider vinegar

Directions:

1. Whisk together honey, ketchup, Worcestershire sauce, sriracha sauce, soy sauce, Dijon mustard and cider vinegar in an airtight container.

2. Cover the container and refrigerate until use. It can last for three–four days.

Whiskey Grill Glaze

Makes: About 1-½ cups

Ingredients:

- ½ tbsp onion powder
- ½ tbsp hot pepper sauce
- ¼ cup whiskey
- 1 beef bouillon cube
- ½ tbsp garlic powder
- ½ cup pineapple juice
- 1 cup packed brown sugar

Directions:

1. Combine onion powder, hot pepper sauce, whiskey, bouillon cube, garlic powder, pineapple juice and brown sugar in a saucepan.

2. Heat the mixture over medium flame and bring to a boil, stirring frequently.

3. Lower the flame and simmer until slightly thick.

4. Turn off the heat and cool completely. Transfer into an airtight container. Refrigerate until use.

Honey-Mustard Glaze

Makes: 5-½ cups

Ingredients:

- 2 cups honey
- 1 cup brown sugar
- 2 cups yellow spicy mustard
- ½ cup pineapple juice

Directions:

1. Whisk together honey, mustard, brown sugar, and pineapple juice in an airtight container. Keep whisking until brown sugar dissolves completely.

2. Cover the container and chill. It can last for two weeks.

3. This glaze goes well with ham. Use it over the ham during the last 30–40 minutes of grilling.

Simple BBQ Glaze

Makes: About 1-½ cups

Ingredients:

- 1 cup ketchup
- 4 tbsp brown sugar
- Salt or to taste
- 6 tbsp cider vinegar
- 4 tbsp Worcestershire sauce
- 1 tsp pepper or to taste

Directions:

1. Whisk together ketchup, brown sugar, salt, cider vinegar, Worcestershire sauce and pepper in a bowl.

2. Keep brushing over the meat and veggies all the way through grilling. This glaze is great for pork and chicken.

Southwest Grilling Glaze

Makes: 1 cup

Ingredients:

- ½ cup butter
- 1 tsp ground cumin
- 1 tsp chopped garlic
- ½ cup tomato puree
- 1 tbsp Better than Bouillon Roasted Beef Base
- ½ tsp ground black pepper

Directions:

1. Add butter into a saucepan. Also add cumin, garlic, tomato puree, Better than Bouillon Roasted Beef Base and place the saucepan over medium flame.
2. Stir often and let it come to a boil. Turn off the heat.
3. Cool completely. Transfer into an airtight container and refrigerate until use.

Watermelon Glaze

Makes: About 1-¼ cups

Ingredients:

- 2 cups watermelon chunks
- ½ jar (from a 12 oz jar) apple jelly
- ½ tsp jalapeño hot sauce
- Juice of ½ lime
- Zest of ½ lime, grated
- 1 tsp red chili flakes
- Salt to taste

Directions:

1. Blend the watermelon cubes in a blender until smooth.

2. Pass the blended watermelon through a strainer placed over a bowl. Discard the watermelon bits in the strainer. You need to use about half a cup of the juice. Freeze the remaining juice or use it in some other recipe.

3. Add apple jelly into a small saucepan and place over low flame. Stir frequently until it melts. Add watermelon juice, lime zest, lime juice, chili flakes, salt and hot sauce and stir.

4. When the mixture is smooth, turn off the heat. Cool completely.

5. Transfer into an airtight container. Refrigerate until use. It can last for two days.

Bourbon Brown Sugar Glaze

Makes: About 4 cups

Ingredients:

- 1 cup packed brown sugar
- 1 cup bourbon whiskey
- 4 tbsp apple cider
- 1 cup apple butter
- ½ cup apple cider vinegar
- 4 tbsp Dijon mustard

Directions:

1. Whisk together brown sugar, apple butter, bourbon whiskey, apple cider, apple cider vinegar and Dijon mustard in a saucepan.

2. Place the saucepan over medium heat and stir frequently until brown sugar dissolves completely.

3. Turn off the heat and cool completely.

4. Transfer into an airtight container.

Chapter 3:
Pork Recipes

Twice Smoked Ham with Sweet Cinnamon Glaze

Preparation time: 10 minutes

Cooking time: About 20 minutes per pound of meat

Cooking method: Smoking

Makes: 4–5 servings

Temperature: 225°F

Pellets: Hickory or maple or mesquite

Ingredients:

- ¼ cup brown sugar
- 1 tbsp Dijon mustard
- 1/8 tsp ground nutmeg
- ¼ tsp ground cinnamon
- ¼ cup pure maple syrup
- 1 ham (4 lbs) spiral cut

Directions:

1. Operate the grill following the instructions of the manufacturer and light up the pellets. Set the grill on 'Smoke' option. Leave the lid open and let it operate for 10 minutes. Set the temperature at 225°F and close the lid to preheat the grill.

2. Keep the ham in a roasting pan and place the pan in the smoking case. Keep the lid of the smoker grill covered and smoke for one–two hours, until the internal temperature of the meat in the thickest part, when measured with a meat thermometer shows 130°F–135°F.

3. To make glaze: Combine brown sugar, Dijon mustard, maple syrup, Dijon mustard, nutmeg and cinnamon in a saucepan.

4. Place the saucepan over medium flame on your stovetop. Stir frequently until brown sugar dissolves completely and the mixture is slightly thick. If the glaze is very thick, add some apple juice or root beer to make it spreadable.

5. Brush some of the glaze all over the ham and place the pan back in the smoking case.

6. Cook until the internal temperature of the meat in the thickest part, when measured with a meat thermometer shows 140°F, basting with the glaze every 10 minutes.

7. Take out the roasting pan from the grill and tent loosely with foil. Let it remain this way for 30 minutes.

8. Serve.

Smoked Carnitas

Preparation time: 10 minutes

Cooking time: 70–80 minutes per pound of meat + braising time

Cooking method: Smoking

Makes: 4 servings

Temperature: 225°F, 350°F and highest setting

Pellets: Hickory

Ingredients:

For pork shoulder:

- 1-½ lbs pork shoulder

- 1 tbsp coarsely ground pepper
- ½ tbsp ground cumin
- 1 tbsp yellow mustard
- 1 tbsp kosher salt
- 1 tbsp paprika
- ½ tbsp chili powder

For braising liquid:

- 2–3 guajillo peppers
- ½ red onion, chopped
- 1 bay leaf
- 1 cup water
- 1 orange, squeezed into juice
- 2 cloves garlic, peeled, chopped
- ½ tsp salt or to taste

To serve:

- Cooked or canned beans
- Cooked rice
- Tortillas
- Chopped onions
- Chopped cilantro

Directions:

1. Operate the grill following the instructions of the manufacturer and light up the pellets. Set the grill on 'Smoke' option. Leave the lid open and let it operate for 10 minutes. Set the temperature at 225°F and close the lid to preheat the grill.

2. Add salt and spices into a spice shaker. Shake until well combined.

3. Smear yellow mustard over the pork shoulder. Sprinkle the spice mixture all over the pork.

4. Place the meat on the grill and set the timer for about two hours.

5. Take out the meat from the grill and place it on your cutting board. Raise the temperature of the grill to 350°F.

6. Remove the meat from the bones and chop into chunks. Place them in a Dutch oven. Pour orange juice into the Dutch oven. Scatter onion, garlic and bay leaf. Drizzle water over the meat. Pour more water if the meat is not covered with water. Close the lid of the Dutch oven.

7. Place it in the smoking case. Set the timer for about 1-½–2 hours. Take out the Dutch oven from the grill and set it aside on your countertop.

8. Raise the temperature of the grill to the highest available temperature. Keep a cast iron skillet inside the smoking case and close the lid of the grill. This is to preheat the skillet.

9. Take out the pork from the Dutch oven and transfer it into a colander. Let any of the cooked liquid drain off.

10. In 10–15 minutes, the skillet should be hot. Place pork in the skillet. Cook for a few minutes until crisp, stirring and breaking while crisping.

11. Serve over tortillas. Also place some rice and beans over the tortillas. Scatter some onion and cilantro on top and serve.

Sweet & Smoky Barbacoa Pulled Pork

Preparation time: 5 minutes + brining time

Cooking time: About 1 ½ hours per pound of meat

Cooking method: Smoking

Makes: 3 servings

Temperature: 225°F

Pellets: Apple

Ingredients:

For brining pork:

- 1 cup apple juice
- ¼ cup salt
- 1/8 tsp chipotle chili powder or more to taste
- ¼ tsp garlic powder

154

- 2 cups Dr. Pepper
- ½ cup brown sugar
- ¼ tsp ground cumin
- 2-½–3 lbs bone-in pork shoulder

For Baracoa sauce:

- ½ can Dr. Pepper
- ½ can red enchilada sauce
- 1/8 tsp chipotle chili powder
- ¼ tsp garlic powder
- ½ can green chilies
- ¼ cup brown sugar
- ¼ tsp ground cumin

For spraying:

- Apple juice

Directions:

1. To make brining liquid: Whisk together apple juice, salt, brown sugar, spices and Dr. Pepper in a bowl.

2. Once brown sugar and salt dissolves completely, place pork in the bowl. It should be immersed in the brining liquid. Set aside for at least 24 hours.

3. Operate the grill following the instructions of the manufacturer and light up the pellets. Set the grill on 'Smoke' option. Leave the lid open and let it operate for 10 minutes. Set the temperature at 180°F and close the lid to preheat the grill for 15 minutes.

4. Remove the pork from the brining liquid and place it on the grill grates with the fat part facing up.

5. Let it smoke for 1-½–2 hours, making sure to spray apple juice over the pork every 50–60 minutes.

6. Raise the temperature of the grill to 250°F.

7. Continue smoking the meat 2-½–3 hours or until the internal temperature of the meat in the thickest part, when measured with a meat thermometer shows 195°F.

Once the meat is at this temperature, when you turn and pull the bone, it will come off easily.

8. Take out the meat from the grill and keep it wrapped with aluminum foil. Cover it now with a towel. Keep the wrapped meat in a cooler for 30–60 minutes.

9. To make barbacoa sauce: Meanwhile, whisk together Dr. Pepper, enchilada sauce, brown sugar, green chilies and spices in a bowl. Keep stirring until brown sugar dissolves completely.

10. Now unwrap and pull the pork into shreds. The bones and fat with cap is to be discarded.

11. Place the pulled pork in the bowl of barbacoa sauce and stir until well combined.

12. Serve with some beans or avocado or any side dish.

Chapter 4:
Beef Recipes

Beef Tenderloin Steaks with Blue Cheese and Peppercorn Butter

Preparation time: 10 minutes

Cooking time: 40 minutes

Cooking method: Grilling

Makes: 2 servings

Temperature: 185°F, 450°F

Pellets: Alder

Ingredients:

- 2 tbsp butter, at room temperature
- 2 small cloves garlic, peeled, minced
- ½ tsp coarsely ground black and green peppercorns
- 2 beef tenderloin steaks (1-¼–1-½ inches thick)
- Steak dry rub, as required
- 1-½ tbsp crumbled blue cheese
- ½ tbsp dry sherry or red wine (optional)
- Salt to taste
- Extra-virgin olive oil, as required

Directions:

1. To make blue cheese and peppercorn butter: Place butter, garlic, peppercorns, blue cheese, sherry and salt in a bowl. Stir until well combined. Cover the bowl and chill.

2. Operate the grill following the instructions of the manufacturer and light up the pellets. Set the grill on 'Smoke' option. Set the temperature at 185°F and close the lid to preheat the grill.

3. Brush oil on the steaks. Sprinkle steak dry rub over it.

4. Place the steaks on the grill grate. Close the lid and set the timer for 30 minutes.

5. When the timer goes off remove the steaks from the grill and place it on a plate.

6. Raise the temperature to 450°F and close the lid to preheat the grill.

7. Place the steaks on the grill grate and set the grill on 'Grill' option. Grill until the way you prefer to be cooked. Turn the steaks a couple of times while grilling.

8. Place a big blob of the blue cheese and peppercorn butter over the steaks. Remove the steaks after a minute and serve.

Grilled Steak Sandwiches

Preparation time: 10 minutes

Cooking time: 15 minutes

Cooking method: Grilling

Makes: 2 servings

Temperature: 425°F

Pellets: Apple or cherry

Ingredients:

- 1-½ tbsp unsalted butter
- ½ green bell pepper, sliced
- 4 oz mozzarella cheese, cut into round slices
- 1 ribeye steak about 1 ½ inches thick

- ½ onion, thinly sliced
- ½ cup crimini mushrooms
- 2 hoagie rolls, slit along the length
- ½ tbsp olive oil
- Steak dry rub, as required

Directions:

1. Operate the grill following the instructions of the manufacturer and light up the pellets. Set the grill on 'Smoke' option. Leave the lid open and let it operate for 10 minutes. Set the temperature to 425°F and preheat for about 15 minutes, keeping the lid closed.

2. Sprinkle a generous amount of steak rub all over the steak.

3. To make compound butter: Place butter in a bowl. Add some steak rub to taste and mix well.

4. Place the steak on the grill grates. Set the grill on 'Grill' option and grill for three minutes. Flip sides and grill the other side for three minutes.

5. Take out the steak from the grill and place on your cutting board. Let it rest for about 10 minutes.

6. Place a cast iron skillet over the grill. Pour olive oil and let it heat for a couple of minutes.

7. Add mushrooms and cook for a couple of minutes. Add onion, bell pepper and half the compound butter and mix well. Cook for a couple of minutes or until the vegetables are tender.

8. Cut the steak into thin slices and stir it into the skillet. Mix well. Stir in remaining compound butter. Turn off the heat.

9. Place the steak mixture in the slit of the hoagie rolls. Place mozzarella cheese slices on top and grill for five–10 minutes. Place them on the top shelf of the grill.

10. Cool for two–three minutes and serve.

Smoked Beef Stew

Preparation time: 20 minutes

Cooking time: 3 hours

Cooking method: Smoking

Makes: 8 servings

Temperature: 275°F

Pellets: Mesquite or oak or hickory

Ingredients:

- 4 lbs stew beef, cut into 1 inch cubes
- ½ cup basic beef rub or any other rub of your choice
- 2 large onions, diced
- 6–8 large potatoes, peeled, diced
- 6–8 large carrots, peeled, diced
- 2 cans (28 oz each) diced tomatoes

- 10 cups beef broth
- 3–4 tbsp cornstarch mixed with ½ cup water

Directions:

1. Sprinkle beef rub all over the stew meat and rub it in.

2. Operate the grill following the instructions of the manufacturer and light up the pellets. Set the grill on 'Smoke' option. Leave the lid open and let it operate for 10 minutes. Set the temperature to 250°F and preheat for about 15 minutes, with the lid closed.

3. Smoke the meat for about two hours.

4. Remove the meat from the smoker. Transfer into a Dutch oven. Add vegetables, tomatoes and broth and stir. Close the lid of the Dutch oven.

5. Place it on the grill grate and cook for about one hour or until the vegetables are tender.

6. During the last 15 minutes of cooking, add the cornstarch mixture. Stir well. Cook for the remaining time.

7. When done, serve hot with crusty bread.

Short Rib Chili

Preparation time: 15 minutes

Cooking time: 4 hours

Cooking method: Smoking

Makes: 8 servings

Temperature: 225°F

Pellets: Maple

Ingredients:

- 4 whole dried guajillo chilies, stemmed, deseeded
- 4 whole dried ancho chilies, stemmed, deseeded
- 4 whole dried chilie de abrol , stemmed, deseeded
- 3 quarts chicken or beef stock
- 8 lbs boneless beef short ribs
- 4 tbsp vegetable oil + extra if required
- 8 cloves garlic, chopped
- 2 sticks cinnamon
- 2 tsp Mexican oregano
- 2 tsp roasted ground coriander
- 2 tsp roasted ground cumin
- Pepper to taste
- 4 chipotle peppers in adobo sauce + 4 teaspoons adobo sauce from the can
- Salt to taste
- 2 large onions, diced
- 2 jalapeños, finely chopped
- 4 bay leaves
- 2 bottles beer

To serve:

- Corn tortillas
- Shredded cheddar cheese

- A handful fresh cilantro, chopped
- 1 onion, chopped
- Lime slices

Directions:

2. Place a skillet over your stovetop, over medium flame. Add all the dried chilies and stir-fry for a couple of minutes, until aromatic.

3. Pour two cups of stock and bring to a boil. Remove the skillet from heat. Cover the pan with a lid.

4. After about 10 minutes, pour the broth along with chilies into a blender. Also add chipotle pepper and four teaspoons adobo sauce into the blender. Blend until smooth.

5. Sprinkle salt and pepper generously over the short ribs.

6. Place a large Dutch oven over medium-high flame on your stovetop. Add some of the vegetable oil. When the oil is heated, cook the short rib in batches until brown. Remove the short ribs and place in a large bowl.

7. Add a little vegetable oil for each batch of short ribs.

8. When the meat is cool enough to handle, chop into bite size chunks.

9. Reduce the heat to medium heat. Add onions into the Dutch oven. Cook until translucent.

10. Stir in garlic, bay leaves, cinnamon, oregano, jalapeños, coriander and cumin and cook for about one minute, until you get a nice aroma.

11. Add beer and stir well. Scrape the bottom of the pot to remove any browned bits that may be stuck. Cook until liquid in the pot reduces to half its original quantity.

12. Add blended ground chili and remaining broth. Add meat back into the pot and stir. The meat should be covered by broth so add broth accordingly. Turn off the heat and do not cover the Dutch oven.

13. Operate the grill following the instructions of the manufacturer and light up the pellets. Set the grill on 'Smoke' option. Set the temperature at 225°F and close the lid to preheat the grill.

14. Shift the Dutch oven on the grill and smoke for three hours or until the meat is very well cooked.

15. Serve in bowls with suggested serving options.

Chapter 5:
Lamb Recipes

Grilled Lamb Kabobs

Preparation time: 15 minutes + chilling time

Cooking time: 10 minutes

Cooking method: Grilling

Makes: 8 servings

Temperature: 400°F

Pellets: Mesquite

Ingredients:

- 1 cup olive oil
- 4 tsp ground black pepper
- 1 tbsp salt
- 1 tbsp minced fresh cilantro
- ¼ cup minced fresh mint
- 1 cup lemon juice
- 2 tsp ground cumin
- 2 tbsp grated lemon zest
- 6 lbs boneless leg of lamb, cut into 2 inch chunks
- 4 red onions, cut each into 8 wedges
- 30 whole dried apricots

To serve: Optional

- Cooked couscous
- Steamed rice
- Cooked quinoa etc.

Directions:

1. Add salt, lemon juice, cumin, cilantro, mint, oil, pepper and lemon zest into a large bowl and stir well.
2. Place lamb in the bowl and turn it around so that lamb is well coated with the mixture.
3. Chill for eight–nine hours.
4. Take out the bowl from the refrigerator and the lamb from the bowl.
5. Thread the lamb pieces onto skewers. Place onion wedges and apricots in between the lamb pieces.
6. Operate the grill following the instructions of the manufacturer and light up the pellets. Set the grill on 'Grill' option. Set the temperature to 400°F and preheat for about 15 minutes. Keep the lid closed while preheating.
7. Place the skewers on the grill grate and grill for 8 to 10 minutes or until the meat is cooked to your preference.

Lamb Stew

Preparation time: 45 minutes

Cooking time: About 1-½–2 hours

Cooking method: Smoking

Makes: 8 servings

Temperature: 450°F

Pellets: Oak

Ingredients:

- 4 tbsp olive oil
- 8 cloves garlic, peeled, chopped
- 4 cups beef stock
- 6 lbs lamb, cut into ½ inch pieces
- ½ cup tomato paste
- 4 tbsp dried thyme
- Salt to taste
- Pepper to taste
- 4 bay leaves
- 24 oz stout beer
- 2 large turnips, diced
- 6 large carrots, diced
- 2 large parsnips, peeled, cut into cubes
- 4 large onions, diced

To serve:

- Mashed potatoes

Directions:

1. Operate the grill following the instructions of the manufacturer and light up the pellets. Set the grill on 'Grill' option. Set the temperature to 450°F and preheat for about 15 minutes. Place a Dutch oven in the grill to preheat. Keep the lid of the grill closed while preheating.

2. Sprinkle salt and pepper over the lamb.

3. Pour oil into the Dutch oven. Let the oil heat. Cook the lamb in batches in the Dutch oven, until brown all over. Remove each batch and place them all in a bowl.

4. Once all the lamb is cooked, add it back into the Dutch oven. Add garlic and stir-fry for a couple of minutes.

5. Stir in tomato paste. After cooking for a minute, pour beer and beef stock. Stir well.

6. Add bay leaves and thyme. Add salt and pepper to taste. Add carrots, parsnip, onions and turnip and stir. Cover the Dutch oven and cook until meat and vegetables are tender. Stir occasionally.

7. Serve stew with mashed potatoes.

Grilled Lamb Burgers with Pickled Onions

Preparation time: 10 minutes

Cooking time: 10 minutes

Cooking method: Grilling

Makes: 8–10 servings

Temperature: 400°F

Pellets: Hickory

Ingredients:

<u>For pickled onions:</u>

- 1 red onion, thinly sliced
- 1 tsp kosher salt
- 12 tbsp lime juice
- 1 tsp raw cane sugar

For burger:

- 2 tbsp olive oil
- 1 lb ground pork
- 2 lbs ground lamb
- ¼ cup finely chopped fresh dill
- 1/3 cup finely chopped fresh mint
- 1/3 cup finely chopped fresh parsley
- 3 tsp ground cumin
- 8 cloves garlic, peeled, minced
- 2 tsp ground coriander
- 1 tsp freshly ground pepper
- 2 tsp kosher salt

To serve:

- Burger buns
- 2 cups herb and garlic yogurt sauce
- Round cucumber slices, as required
- Round tomato slices, as required
- Lettuce leaves, as required

Directions:

1. To make pickled onions: Combine lime juice, onions, sugar and salt in a bowl. Stir well. Cover the bowl and set aside on your countertop for two hours. Stir every 15 minutes. Chill until use.

2. Place a skillet over medium flame, on your stovetop. Pour oil and let it heat. Add onions and sauté until translucent. Turn off the heat and let it cool.

3. Place meat in a large bowl along with fresh herbs, salt, spices and onions. Mix using your hands until just combined. Make sure that you do not mix for long lest the meat will get tough.

4. Divide the mixture into eight–10 equal portions and shape into patties.

5. Operate the grill following the instructions of the manufacturer and light up the pellets. Set the grill on 'Grill' option. Set the temperature at 400°F and close the lid to preheat the grill.

6. Place the burgers on the grill grate and grill for two–five minutes, depending on how you like it cooked. Flip sides and grill the other side for two–five minutes.

7. Remove the burgers and place them on a plate.

8. Place the burger buns on the grill and toast them to the desired doneness.

9. Place burgers on the bottom half of the buns. Spread some herb and garlic yogurt sauce over it. Place cucumber and tomato slices over the burgers. Cover with the top half of the buns and serve.

Chapter 6:
Poultry Recipes

Alabama Chicken Leg Quarters

Preparation time: 15 minutes

Cooking time: 1-½–2 hours

Cooking method: Grilling

Makes: 2–3 servings

Temperature: 275°F – 300°F

Pellets: Hickory or apple or cherry or alder

Ingredients:

- 2–3 chicken leg quarters (together, the leg and thigh), trimmed of extra skin and fat
- ¼ cup all-purpose rub

- ½ bottle Italian dressing

For Alabama sauce:

- 1 cup mayonnaise
- ½ tbsp sugar
- Juice of a lemon
- ¼ cup apple cider vinegar
- ½ tsp horseradish
- 1 tbsp all-purpose rub

Directions:

1. Take a Ziploc bag and place the chicken in it. Drizzle Italian dressing over it. Seal the bag and place it in a bowl. Chill for four–eight hours.

2. Operate the grill following the instructions of the manufacturer and light up the pellets. Set the grill on 'Smoke' option. Leave the lid open and let it operate for 10 minutes. Set the temperature at 275°F–300°F and preheat the grill for 15 minutes. Close the lid while preheating.

3. Now take out the chicken from the Ziploc bag and sprinkle rub all over the chicken.

4. Place the chicken on the grill, with the skin side facing up. Cook for about 35–45 minutes, keeping a watch over the chicken as it can get burnt. The internal temperature of the meat in the thickest part should be 170°F–180°F.

5. Turn the chicken over and cook for another 40–45 minutes or until chicken is cooked through. Turn the chicken a few times if necessary.

6. Drizzle Alabama sauce over the leg quarters and serve.

Smoked Boneless Chicken Breast

Preparation time: 30 minutes

Cooking time: 1-½ hours

Cooking method: Smoking

Makes: 8 servings

Temperature: 250°F

Pellets: Hickory or apple or cherry or alder

Ingredients:

- 12 boneless, skinless chicken breasts
- 1-½ cups chicken rub of your choice

For brine:

- 4 quarts water
- 1 cup white sugar
- Juice of 1 lemon
- 1 cup table salt
- ½ cup soy sauce
- 2 tbsp olive oil

Directions:

1. Pour water into a large container or bucket. Stir in salt, sugar and olive oil.

2. Once sugar and salt dissolves fully, stir in soy sauce and lemon juice.

3. Place the chicken breasts in it. The brine should cover the chicken.

4. Place the container on your countertop and let it sit for about 30 minutes. The longer the better. Four–five hours is ideal. If you are keeping the chicken in brine for more than 30 minutes, place the container in the refrigerator.

5. Now remove the chicken pieces from the brine and dry them by patting with paper towels. Dry one chicken breast at a time and place them on a baking sheet.

6. Sprinkle rub all over the chicken breasts.

7. Just before you remove the chicken from the refrigerator, prepare your grill.

8. Operate the grill following the instructions of the manufacturer and light up the pellets. Set the grill on 'Smoke' option. Leave the lid open and let it operate for 10 minutes. Set the temperature at 250°F and preheat the grill for 15 minutes. Close the lid while preheating.

9. Place the chicken on the grill and close the lid. Set the timer 45 minutes. Do not remove the lid until 45 minutes are up.

10. Check the internal temperature of the grill. It should be around 165°F else increase it to 200°F.

11. Continue cooking the chicken for 15 minutes, with the lid closed.

12. Once grilled, take out the chicken from the grill and let it rest for five–10 minutes before serving.

Grilled Parmesan Garlic Chicken Wings

Preparation time: 10 minutes

Cooking time: 25 minutes

Cooking method: Grilling

Makes: 2 servings

Temperature: 400°F

Pellets: Competition blend

Ingredients:

- 2 tbsp butter
- 2 cloves garlic, peeled, chopped
- ¼ cup grated parmesan cheese
- Chicken rub of your choice, as required

- 2 lbs chicken wings
- 1 tbsp olive oil
- 1 tbsp chopped parsley

Directions:

1. Place chicken wings on a baking sheet. Dry them by patting with paper towels. Sprinkle chicken rub over it.

2. Operate the grill following the instructions of the manufacturer and light up the pellets. Set the grill on 'Grill' option. Set the temperature at 400°F and preheat the grill for 15 minutes. Close the lid while preheating.

3. Remove the wings from the baking sheet and place them on the grill grate. Grill the wings for about 20–25 minutes or until light brown. Turn the wings after every five minutes.

4. Take out the wings from the grill and place it back on the baking sheet.

5. Keep the baking sheet in the smoking case so that it remains warm.

6. To make garlic butter: Place a cast iron skillet over the grill. Add butter and olive oil. Once butter melts, add garlic and sauté for a few minutes until aromatic.

7. Take out the wings from the smoking case and place the wings in a bowl. Drizzle the garlic butter over the wings.

8. Sprinkle cheese and parsley over the wings and toss well.

9. Serve with some more cheese.

Buffalo Chicken Egg Rolls

Preparation time: 20 minutes

Cooking time: 1 hour and 15 minutes

Cooking method: Grilling

Makes: 2 servings

Temperature: 200°F

Pellets: Classic blend

Ingredients:

- 2 tbsp crumbled blue cheese
- ½ lb skinless, boneless chicken breasts
- 4 egg roll wrappers
- ¼ tsp BBQ spice rub or more if desired

- 2 scallions, thinly sliced
- 1 cup vegetable oil or more if required
- 2 tbsp buffalo sauce
- 2 oz cream cheese, at room temperature
- 1 tsp minced jalapeño pepper
- ½ small red bell pepper, chopped
- 2 tbsp sour cream

Directions:

1. Operate the grill following the instructions of the manufacturer and light up the pellets. Set the grill on 'Grill' option. Set the temperature at 200°F and preheat the grill for 15 minutes. Close the lid while preheating.

2. Sprinkle BBQ spice rub over the chicken and place them on the grill. Cook for about an hour with the lid closed.

3. Take out the chicken from the grill and place it on a plate. When cool enough to handle, shred the chicken.

4. To make filling: Combine cream cheese, sour cream, buffalo sauce and blue cheese in a bowl. Beat with an electric hand mixer until well combined.

5. Stir in jalapeño, scallions, red bell pepper and chicken.

6. To make egg rolls: Place an egg roll wrapper on your countertop. Place three tablespoons of the filling on the center of the wrapper.

7. Have some warm water ready in a bowl. First fold the bottom part of the wrapper over the filling. Next fold the left and the right sides over the filling. Brush the top part of the unfolded wrapper with some warm water.

8. Now roll the wrapper along with the filling and press the top edge to seal.

9. Place it on the baking sheet. Repeat the same process with the remaining wrappers.

10. Place a Dutch oven on the grill. Pour one–two cups of oil in the Dutch oven. Raise the temperature of the grill to 425°F

11. When the oil is well heated but not smoking, carefully slide the filled egg rolls in the oil, a few at a time. Cook until golden brown all over. Fry the remaining egg rolls similarly.

12. Remove with a slotted spoon and place on a plate lined with paper towels.

13. Serve with some more buffalo sauce.

Chapter 7:
Seafood Recipes

Smoked Buttery Shrimp

Preparation time: 20 minutes

Cooking time: 25 minutes

Cooking method: Smoking

Makes: 10 servings

Temperature: 275°F

Pellets: Pecan

Ingredients:

- 30 large shrimp, deveined, peeled if desired
- 2 cloves garlic, peeled, minced
- 2 tbsp seasoning of your choice
- 1 cup butter, melted
- 4 sticks rosemary
- Juice of ½ lemon

Directions:

1. Sprinkle seasoning all over the shrimp.

2. Combine garlic and melted butter in a bowl.

3. Place shrimp in six rows in the foil pan. Drizzle garlic butter over the shrimp. Drizzle lemon juice over the shrimp. Place rosemary sticks, in between the rows.

4. Operate the grill following the instructions of the manufacturer and light up the pellets. Set the grill on 'Grill' option. Set the temperature at 275°F and preheat the grill for 15 minutes. Close the lid while preheating.

5. Place the salmon on the grill grate and set the timer for 20–25 minutes. When the shrimp are cooked, it will look somewhat orange in color. Do not overcook.

6. Serve hot with a side dish of your choice.

Caribbean Curry Grilled Lobsters with Garlic Lime Asparagus

Preparation time: 25 minutes

Cooking time: 20 minutes

Cooking method: Grilling

Makes: 4 servings

Temperature: 425°F

Pellets: Oak

Ingredients:

- ½ cup butter, softened
- ½ tbsp minced ginger
- 2 cloves, peeled, minced
- Zest of ½ lime, grated

- Juice of ½ lime
- ¼ tsp turmeric powder
- 1 tbsp minced cilantro leaves
- ¼ tsp curry powder or to taste
- 1/8 tsp ground cayenne pepper
- 1 tbsp finely chopped chives
- 2 live lobsters (about ¾ lb)

For garlic lime asparagus:

- 1 tbsp olive oil
- ½ bunch asparagus, remove the hard ends
- 1 clove garlic, peeled, minced
- Lime wedges to serve
- 1 tbsp olive oil
- Zest of ½ lime, grated
- Chopped cilantro to garnish

Directions:

1. Place a pot of water with some salt in it over high flame on your stovetop. Let it come to a boil.

2. Meanwhile, make the curry butter by combining garlic, ginger, butter, lime zest, lime juice, herbs and spices in a bowl. Mix until well combined.

3. To prepare lobsters: Keep the lobsters on your cutting board. Cut the lobsters from the tip of a chef's knife at the point just below the meeting point of the claws up to the head and place it in the boiling water, one at a time. Cover the pot and cook for two minutes. Turn off the heat. Remove the lobsters from the pot and place it in the ice bath. The color of the lobsters will be red and flesh will be opaque.

4. Now cut with a knife through the body and tail as well.

5. Place asparagus, lime zest and garlic in a bowl and toss well. Drizzle oil over it and toss well.

6. Operate the grill following the instructions of the manufacturer and light up the pellets. Set the grill on 'Grill' option. Set the temperature at 425°F and preheat the grill for 15 minutes. Close the lid while preheating.

7. Lay the lobsters with the flesh side facing down, on the grill grate. Also place the asparagus next to the lobsters. Spread a little of the curry butter over the lobsters. Set the timer for eight minutes.

8. Flip the lobsters after four minutes of grilling. Spread some more of the curry butter on the lobsters.

9. Once cooked through, remove lobsters and asparagus and serve with lime wedges.

10. Garnish with cilantro. If there is any curry butter remaining, spoon it over the lobsters and serve.

Smoked Seafood Paella

Preparation time: 30 minutes

Cooking time: 45–60 minutes

Cooking method: Smoking

Makes: 3 servings

Temperature: 400°F

Pellets: Oak

Ingredients:

- 4 cups chicken broth
- 2 tbsp extra-virgin olive oil + extra to drizzle
- ½ medium yellow onion, diced
- 1 cup Arborio rice or any other short grain rice of your choice
- ½ lb clams or mussels or mixture of both
- 1 lb shrimp with shells
- 1 lemon, quartered
- ½ tsp saffron threads
- ¼ lb dried chorizo, sliced
- 1 clove garlic, peeled, minced
- ½ cup frozen peas
- A handful flat-leaf parsley
- Salt to taste

Directions:

2. Operate the grill following the instructions of the manufacturer and light up the pellets. Set the grill on 'Smoke' option. Leave the lid open and let it operate for 10 minutes.

3. Set the temperature at 400°F and preheat the grill for 15 minutes. Close the lid while preheating.

4. Pour stock and saffron in the saucepan and place it on the grill. Stir occasionally.

5. Pour oil into the paella pan and place it over the grill as well.

6. Once oil is heated, add onion and chorizo and sauté until onion turns translucent.

7. Stir in the garlic and cover the pan. Continue cooking for a couple of minutes.

8. Add rice and salt to taste. Stir for a couple of minutes until rice is well coated with oil.

9. Once rice is well coated with oil, spread it evenly, all over the pan. Pour some of the stock over the rice. It should barely cover the rice. The rice is not to be stirred.

10. Close the lid of the grill and let it cook for about 10–12 minutes.

11. Spread peas over the rice. Spread the seafood over the rice, with the seams touching the rice.

12. Drizzle some more of the stock over the seafood layer.

13. Close the lid once again and cook until the stock has been absorbed. The clams and mussels would have opened by now. Discard those that are not opened.

14. Check if the rice is cooked. If cooked, remove the pan from the grill. If it is not cooked, drizzle some more stock into the pan and cook until rice is tender.

15. Garnish with parsley and lemon quarters and serve.

Chapter 8:
Appetizers and Sides Recipes

Smokey Meatballs

Preparation time: 20 minutes

Cooking time: 30–40 minutes

Cooking method: Smoking

Makes: 15–20 servings

Temperature: 225°F

Pellets: Hickory or oak or pecan

Ingredients:

- 2 lbs lean ground beef
- 1 cup finely grated parmesan cheese
- 2 tbsp garlic powder
- 2 tbsp brown sugar
- 1 tsp smoked paprika
- ½ tsp chipotle chili powder
- 2 tbsp onion powder
- 2 tsp kosher salt or to taste
- ½ tsp chili powder
- ¼ tsp ground cumin
- 1 cup finely diced onions
- 2 large eggs, lightly beaten
- 1 cup BBQ sauce
- 2/3 cup breadcrumbs
- 1 cup shredded old cheddar cheese or Asiago cheese
- Small cubes of old cheddar cheese or Asiago cheese (1/3 inch cubes), as required
- 2 jalapeños, finely chopped
- ¼ cup Worcestershire sauce

Directions:

1. Combine beef, spices, parmesan cheese, brown sugar onions, eggs, breadcrumbs, shredded cheddar cheese, jalapeños, salt and Worcestershire sauce in a bowl.

2. Do not over mix.

3. Make small meatballs of the mixture, by stuffing a cube of cheddar cheese in each meatball.

4. Place meatballs on a baking sheet or pan lined with parchment paper.

5. Operate the grill following the instructions of the manufacturer and light up the pellets. Set the grill on 'Smoke' option. Leave the lid open and let it operate for 10 minutes.

6. Set the temperature at 225°F and preheat the grill for 15 minutes. Close the lid while preheating.

7. Place the baking sheet on the bottom grill grate and close the lid. Smoke for 30 minutes. Baste the meatballs with BBQ sauce and smoke for 30 minutes.

8. Increase the temperature of the grill to 350°F. baste the meatballs with BBQ sauce once again and smoke for 20–30 minutes or until the internal temperature of the meatball shows 160 °F.

Smoked Hummus with Roasted Vegetables

Preparation time: 5 minutes

Cooking time: 40 minutes

Cooking method: Smoking

Makes: 12 servings

Temperature: 180°F

Pellets: Hickory

Ingredients:

For hummus:

- 3 cups cooked or canned chickpeas
- 2 tbsp minced garlic
- Salt to taste
- 2/3 cup tahini
- ¼ cup extra-virgin olive oil
- ½ cup lemon juice

For roasted vegetables:

- 2 red onions, sliced
- 4 cups cauliflower florets
- 4 cups whole Portobello mushrooms
- 4 cups cubed butternut squash
- 4 cups fresh Brussels sprouts
- Salt to taste
- ½ cup extra-virgin olive oil
- Pepper to taste

Directions:

1. Operate the grill following the instructions of the manufacturer and light up the pellets. Set the grill on 'Smoke' option. Set the temperature at 180°F and preheat the grill for 15 minutes. Close the lid while preheating.

2. Spread the chickpeas evenly on a baking sheet.

3. Place the baking sheet on the grill grate and close the lid. Set the timer for 15–20 minutes. Remove the baking sheet from the grill and let the chickpeas cool for a few minutes. Increase the temperature of the grill to 500°F and let it preheat.

4. Transfer the chickpeas into a food processor bowl. Also add garlic, tahini, lemon juice, salt and olive oil and process until well combined and the texture you desire is achieved.

5. Remove hummus into a bowl.

6. To roast vegetables: Place all the vegetables in a roasting pan. Drizzle olive oil over it and toss well. Spread the vegetables in the pan and place it in the grill

7. Roast the vegetables for 15 to 20 minutes or until the vegetables are tender.

8. To serve: Scatter roasted vegetables over the hummus.

9. You can serve it as an appetizer with vegetable sticks or pita bread sticks or with tortilla chips.

10. You can serve it as a side with some grilled meat.

Salmon Cakes

Preparation time: 20 minutes

Cooking time: 1 hour

Cooking method: Grilling

Makes: 8 servings

Temperature: 275°F

Pellets: Maple

Ingredients:

For salmon cakes:

- 4 lbs salmon
- Ground black pepper to taste
- 2 stalks celery, finely chopped
- 2 tbsp finely chopped fresh dill or 1 tsp dried dill
- Salt to taste
- 4 large eggs
- 1 small onion, finely chopped
- 2 red bell peppers, finely chopped
- 2 tsp grated lemon zest
- 3 tbsp breadcrumbs
- 6 tbsp extra-virgin olive oil

Directions:

1. Operate the grill following the instructions of the manufacturer and light up the pellets. Set the grill on 'Grill' option. Set the temperature at 275°F and preheat the grill for 15 minutes. Close the lid while preheating.

2. Sprinkle salt and pepper over the salmon and place them on the grill grate. Cook until the internal temperature of the salmon when measured with a meat thermometer shows 120°F. Take out the salmon from the grill. Place salmon in a bowl and let it cool.

3. Flake the fish with a fork. Mix in onions, bell pepper, celery, breadcrumbs, dill, salt, pepper and lemon zest.

4. Add eggs and mix until well combined.

5. Make 16 equal portions of the mixture and shape into patties.

6. Raise the temperature of the grill to 375°F. Place a cast-iron skillet on the grill. Keep the lid closed and allow it to preheat.

7. Add 2–3 tablespoons oil into the skillet. Once the oil is heated, place a few cakes in the pan and cook until golden brown on both the sides. Remove the cakes with a slotted spoon and place on a plate lined with paper towels.

8. Cook the remaining cakes similarly, add some oil each time.

9. Serve hot with a dip of your choice.

Bacon Onion Rings

Preparation time: 10 minutes

Cooking time: 1-½ hours

Cooking method: Grilling

Makes: 3 servings

Temperature: 275°F

Pellets: Mesquite

Ingredients:

- 8 strips bacon or more if required
- ½ tbsp chili garlic sauce
- ½ tsp honey
- 1 Vidalia onion, cut into ½ inch thick round slices
- ½ tbsp yellow mustard

Directions:

1. Separate the onion rings such that each ring has two onions.

2. Wrap a strip of bacon on each set of rings. Use more bacon strips if required, especially if the onion rings are large in size. Fasten the ends with skewers.

3. Operate the grill following the instructions of the manufacturer and light up the pellets. Set the grill on 'Grill' option. Set the temperature at 400°F and preheat the grill for 15 minutes. Close the lid while preheating.

4. Combine honey, chili garlic sauce and mustard in a bowl. Brush this mixture over the bacon.

5. Place bacon onion rings on the grill grate and grill for about 45 minutes. Flip sides and cook for another 45 minutes or until bacon is golden brown.

Smoked Potatoes

Preparation time: 15 minutes

Cooking time: 2–3 hours

Cooking method: Smoking

Makes: 8–10 servings

Temperature: 375°F

Pellets: Oak

Ingredients:

- 8 large russet potatoes, peeled, cut into 1 inch chunks
- 1 tsp kosher salt or to taste
- Freshly ground pepper to taste

- BBQ rub of your choice or any other seasoning of your choice (optional)
- 4 tbsp olive oil

Directions:

1. Operate the grill following the instructions of the manufacturer and light up the pellets. Set the grill on 'Smoke' option. Set the temperature at 375°F and preheat the grill for 15 minutes. Close the lid while preheating.

2. Place potatoes in a bowl. Drizzle oil over it. Sprinkle salt and pepper and toss well. Sprinkle any other seasoning if using and toss well.

3. Place potatoes on a large sheet of aluminum foil. Wrap the potatoes with foil and place it in the grill.

4. Set the timer for two–three hours or until the potatoes are fork tender.

5. Sprinkle some fresh herbs of your choice over the smoked potatoes and serve.

Glazed Grilled Carrots

Preparation time: 10 minutes

Cooking time: 25 hours

Cooking method: Grilled

Makes: 8 servings

Temperature: 180°F

Pellets: Apple or cherry

Ingredients:

- 20–25 medium carrots, trimmed, halved lengthwise
- 4 tbsp balsamic vinegar
- 2 tbsp dark brown sugar
- 1 clove garlic, very thinly sliced
- 4 tbsp vegetable oil + extra for the carrots
- Salt to taste
- 2 tbsp soy sauce
- 1 tsp finely chopped fresh rosemary
- 2 tsp freshly grated ginger
- 2 green onions, thinly sliced

Directions:

1. Operate the grill following the instructions of the manufacturer and light up the pellets. Set the grill on 'Grill' option. Set the temperature at 180°F and preheat the grill for 15 minutes. Close the lid while preheating.

2. Place carrots in a bowl. Drizzle oil over it. Sprinkle salt and toss well.

3. Place the carrots on the grill. Cover and grill until the carrots are tender and can be pierced easily with a fork. Turn the carrots every five–six minutes to ensure even grilling.

4. Meanwhile, combine vinegar, brown sugar, garlic, four tablespoons oil, salt, soy sauce, rosemary and ginger in a bowl.

5. Place carrots in the bowl of sauce mixture and toss well. Garnish with green onions and serve.

Herb-infused Mashed Potatoes

Preparation time: 20 minutes

Cooking time: 1 hour

Cooking method: Grilling

Makes: 4 servings

Temperature: 350°F

Pellets: Cherry

Ingredients:

- 2-¼ lbs russet potatoes, peeled, cut into 1 inch cubes
- 1 cup heavy cream
- 2 sprigs fresh thyme, chopped + extra to garnish
- 1 sprig fresh rosemary, chopped
- 3 sage leaves

- 1 large clove garlic, peeled, sliced
- Kosher salt to taste
- ¾ cup water
- 3–4 whole peppercorns
- 1 stick unsalted butter, softened
- Freshly ground pepper to taste

Directions:

1. Operate the grill following the instructions of the manufacturer and light up the pellets. Set the grill on 'Grill' option. Set the temperature at 350°F and preheat the grill for 15 minutes. Close the lid while preheating.

2. Place potatoes in an oven proof container and pour water over it.

3. Place the container in the grill and cover the lid. Cook until the potatoes are fork tender.

4. Stir together cream, peppercorns, fresh herbs and garlic in an ovenproof saucepan. Place the saucepan on the grill along with the potatoes, during the last 15 minutes of cooking.

5. Remove both the containers from the grill.

6. Drain off the water from the potatoes. Mash the potatoes with a potato masher.

7. Strain the cream mixture and discard the herbs. Add the strained mixture into the mashed potatoes. Add butter, pepper and salt and mix well.

8. Serve.

Grilled Sweet Potatoes with Honey Glaze

Preparation time: 10 minutes

Cooking time: 20–25 minutes

Cooking method: Grilling

Makes: 8 servings

Temperature: 350°F

Pellets: Apple or cherry or pecan

Ingredients:

- 4 large sweet potatoes, scrubbed, parboiled for a couple of minutes
- 4 tbsp honey
- Olive oil, to brush

Directions:

1. Cool the sweet potatoes completely and cut into ¾ inch thick slices.

2. Operate the grill following the instructions of the manufacturer and light up the pellets. Set the grill on 'Grill' option. Set the temperature at 350°F and preheat the grill for 15 minutes. Close the lid while preheating.

3. Brush oil over the sweet potato slices and place them on a grill.

4. Brush honey over the slices during the last couple of minutes of grilling.

5. Serve hot.

Chapter 9:
Vegetarian Recipes

Smoked Grilled Cheese Sandwich

Preparation time: 10 minutes

Cooking time: 10 minutes

Cooking method: Grilling

Makes: 4 servings

Temperature: 350°F

Pellets: Mixture of maple, cherry and alder or competition blend

Ingredients:

- 8 slices sourdough bread or any other bread slices of your choice
- 4 slices pepper Jack cheese
- 4 slices cheddar cheese
- Butter, softened, as required

Directions:

1. Operate the grill following the instructions of the manufacturer and light up the pellets. Select 'Grill' option. Set the temperature at 375°F and close the lid to preheat the grill.

2. Place one each of Jack and cheddar cheese slices in between two slices of bread. In all you get four sandwiches.

3. Place the sandwiches on the grill and cook for three–five minutes on each side or to the desired doneness.

4. Cut into desired shape. These sandwiches go well with tomato soup.

Grilled Cabbage with Blue Cheese Dressing

Preparation time: 10 minutes

Cooking time: 25 minutes

Cooking method: Grilling

Makes: 8–10 servings

Temperature: 350 °F

Pellets: Apple or cherry or competition blend

Ingredients:

- 8 oz blue cheese, crumbled
- 1 cup sour cream
- Kosher salt to taste
- 4 tbsp extra-virgin olive oil
- Freshly ground pepper to taste
- 2 cups cherry tomatoes, cut into 2 halves if desired
- 1 cup mayonnaise
- 2 tbsp lemon juice
- 2 medium head cabbages, cut into 6 wedges each (do not remove the core)
- ½ cup scallions
- 1 cup bacon, cooked, crumbled (optional)

Directions:

1. Combine blue cheese, mayonnaise, salt, pepper, lemon juice and sour cream in a bowl. Mash the cheese and mix until well combined. Set aside.

2. Operate the grill following the instructions of the manufacturer and light up the pellets. Select 'Grill' option. Set the temperature at 375°F and close the lid to preheat the grill.

3. Grease the grill grate.

4. Place cabbage on the grill and close the lid. Cook until charred. Turn the cabbage to the next side and grill the second side until charred. Similarly turn the cabbage once again and grill the last side until charred. By now it would have been cooked inside as well.

5. Place the grilled cabbage wedges in a bowl. Drizzle oil over the cabbage. Toss well. Sprinkle salt and pepper and toss again.

6. Drizzle blue cheese sauce over it. Top with scallions, tomatoes and bacon if using and serve.

Smoked Pumpkin Soup

Preparation time: 10 minutes

Cooking time: 2 hours

Cooking method: Smoking

Makes: 8 servings

Temperature: 300°F

Pellets: Apple or cherry

Ingredients:

- 2 pumpkins
- 4 cloves garlic, peeled
- 8 cups vegetable stock or water mixed with vegetable bouillon cubes
- 2 onions, chopped
- 2 cups heavy cream
- Salt to taste
- Pepper to taste
- 2 tbsp olive oil

Directions:

1. Cut the pumpkin into two halves. Remove the seeds and the membranes from the pumpkin. Now remove the seeds from the membrane and discard the membrane.
2. Place the seeds on a baking sheet.
3. Operate the grill following the instructions of the manufacturer and light up the pellets. Set the grill on 'Smoke' option. Leave the lid open and let it operate for 10 minutes. Set the temperature at 300°F and close the lid to preheat the grill.
4. Place pumpkins on the grill. Also place the baking sheet on the grill along with the pumpkins. Close the lid and smoke the pumpkins for 1-½ hours.
5. Remove the pumpkins and the seeds from the grill and let it cool.
6. Scoop the pumpkin flesh.
7. Place a soup pot on the grill. Add oil and let it heat. Add onion and garlic and cook until onion turns translucent.
8. Add the scooped pumpkin and stock and mix well. Let it cook for 15 minutes.
9. Remove the pot from the grill and blend the soup with an immersion blender until smooth. Add heavy cream and stir.
10. Add salt and pepper to taste.
11. Ladle into soup bowls and serve.

Spicy Bean Burgers

Preparation time: 20 minutes

Cooking time: 10 minutes

Cooking method: Grilling

Makes: 8 servings

Temperature: 350 °F

Pellets: Apple or cherry

Ingredients:

- 2 tbsp olive oil + extra to brush
- 2 cloves garlic, crushed or minced
- 2 tsp ground coriander

- 2 tsp ground cumin
- 2 small onions, finely chopped
- 8 oz mushrooms, finely chopped
- 2 red chilies, deseeded, finely chopped
- Pepper to taste
- 2 cans (15.5 oz each) red kidney beans, drained, rinsed
- A handful fresh cilantro, chopped
- Salt to taste

To serve:
- Burger buns, split
- Toppings of your choice

Directions:

1. Place a pan over medium flame on your stovetop. Add oil and let it heat.
2. Once oil is heated, add mushrooms and cook for a few minutes until dry.
3. Add onion and garlic and sauté for a few minutes until onions are soft.
4. Stir in the spices and cook for a few seconds. Turn off the heat.
5. Mash the beans in a large bowl. Add onion mixture, red chili, salt and cilantro. Mix well. Taste and adjust the seasonings if required.
6. Divide the mixture into eight–10 equal portions and shape into patties.
7. Operate the grill following the instructions of the manufacturer and light up the pellets. Set the grill on the 'Grill' option. Set the temperature at 350°F and close the lid to preheat the grill.
8. Grease the grill grate.
9. Place the burgers on the grill grate and grill for four–five minutes, depending on how you like them cooked. Flip sides and grill the other side for four–five minutes.
10. Remove the burgers and place them on a plate.
11. Place the burger buns on the grill and toast them to the desired doneness.
12. Place burgers on the bottom half of the buns. Place toppings of your choice. Cover with the top half of the buns and serve.

Chapter 10:
Desserts

Quick N' Easy Pear Cobbler

Preparation time: 10 minutes

Cooking time: 40 minutes

Cooking method: Grilling

Makes: 4–6 servings

Temperature: 350°F

Pellets: Maple or fruitwood

Ingredients:

- 1 large can pear halves in syrup
- ½ cup whole milk

- ¼ tsp vanilla extract
- ½ cup butter
- Brown sugar to sprinkle
- ½ cup flour
- ½ cup sugar
- Cranberries to top, as required

Directions:

1. Operate the grill following the instructions of the manufacturer and light up the pellets. Set the grill on 'Grill' option. Set the temperature at 350°F and preheat the grill for 15 minutes. Close the lid while preheating.

2. Meanwhile, grease a baking dish with some oil or cooking spray.

3. Combine flour, vanilla, sugar and milk in a bowl. Stir until sugar dissolves completely.

4. Place butter in an ovenproof pan and place it on the grill. Once butter melts, take out the pan from the grill.

5. Spoon the batter into the pan and lay the pear halves on the batter. Place cranberries over the pears. Top with brown sugar.

6. Place the pan on the grill and set the timer for 30–40 minutes or until golden brown on top. Keep the lid closed while grilling.

7. Slice and serve warm with vanilla ice cream.

Chocolate Chip & English Toffee Cookies

Preparation time: 25 minutes

Cooking time: 45 minutes

Cooking method: Smoking

Makes: 8–10 servings

Temperature: 275°F, 375°F

Pellets: Cherry

Ingredients:

- ½ cup broken pretzels
- 6 tbsp granulated sugar
- ½ tsp vanilla bean paste
- 1-½ cups all-purpose flour
- ¼ tsp apple pie spice
- ½ tsp smoked salt
- ½ cup milk chocolate chips
- ½ cup semi-sweet chocolate chips
- ¼ cup English toffee bits
- ½ cup butter, softened
- 1 egg, at room temperature
- ½ tsp baking soda
- 5.5 oz caramel bits

Directions:

1. Operate the grill following the instructions of the manufacturer and light up the pellets. Set the grill on 'Smoke' option. Set the temperature at 275°F and preheat the grill for 15 minutes. Close the lid while preheating.

2. Place pretzels on a baking sheet and spread it evenly. Place the baking sheet on the grill and set the timer for about 40–45 minutes.

3. Let the pretzels cool completely. Increase the temperature of the grill to 375°F. close the lid and preheat for 15 minutes.

4. Meanwhile, add butter and sugar into a mixing bowl of the stand mixer. Fit the paddle attachment and set on medium speed. Mix until light and creamy.

5. With the mixer running, add egg and vanilla and beat until well incorporated.

6. Combine baking soda, smoked salt, flour and apple pie spice in a bowl.

7. Set the mixer on low speed and add the flour mixture into the mixing bowl. Mix until just combined making sure not to over-mix.

8. Add both the chocolate chips, toffee bits and caramel bits and fold gently.

9. Using a cookie scoop, scoop out the cookie dough and place on a baking sheet lined with parchment paper. Leave 2-½–3 inches gap between the cookies.

10. Keep the baking sheet on the grill grate. Close the lid and set timer for 10–12 minutes or until light golden brown on the edges.

11. Turn the baking sheet after about six–seven minutes of baking.

12. The cookies will be slightly soft in the center.

13. Cool the cookies on a cooling rack.

14. You can serve them now or transfer into an airtight container. Consume within five days.

Peppermint Ice Cream with Smoked Hot Fudge

Preparation time: 30 minutes

Cooking time: 45 minutes + freezing time

Cooking method: Smoking

Makes: 6–8 servings

Temperature: 300°F

Pellets: Hickory

Ingredients:

For ice cream:

- 6 cups half and half
- 2/3 cup granulated sugar
- 1 tsp vanilla extract

- 2 cups crushed peppermint candies, divided
- 16 egg yolks
- 1 tsp peppermint extract
- 2 tsp kosher salt

For fudge:

- 2 cups heavy cream
- 16 oz semi-sweet chocolate
- 2 tbsp Kahlua or dark rum (optional)

Directions:

2. Pour half and half into a saucepan. Place the saucepan over medium flame. When bubbles are visible around the edges, turn off the heat.

3. Place egg yolks and sugar in a bowl and whisk until well incorporated.

4. Add a little of the half and half, whisking all the while.

5. Pour rest of the half and half, whisking all the time while adding.

6. Pour this mixture into the saucepan. Place the saucepan over low flame. Stir constantly until thick and it can coat the back of a spoon. It should take around five minutes. It should not begin to form curds. If it does, immediately take the saucepan off from heat.

7. Place a wire mesh strainer over a bowl. Pour the mixture into the strainer and strain it into the bowl. Discard solids if any.

8. Add kosher salt, vanilla extract and peppermint extract and stir until well combined.

9. Cover the bowl with cling wrap and chill the ice cream in the refrigerator or on an ice bath.

10. Pour chilled mixture into an ice cream maker and churn the ice cream following the manufacturer's instructions.

11. Add half the peppermint candies during the last five minutes of churning.

12. Transfer into a freezer safe container and freeze until firm.

13. To make smoked hot fudge: Operate the grill following the instructions of the manufacturer and light up the pellets. Set the grill on 'Smoke' option. Set the

temperature at 300°F and preheat the grill for 15 minutes. Close the lid while preheating.

14. Pour heavy cream into an ovenproof saucepan. Place the saucepan on the grill. Smoke the cream, with the lid closed for about 10–12 minutes.

15. Lower the temperature of the grill to 180°F. While the grill is cooling, add rum and chocolate into the saucepan of cream and whisk well. Close the lid and smoke for 10 minutes.

16. Whisk well.

17. Serve ice cream in bowls. Top with fudge and remaining peppermint and serve.

Chapter 11:

Tips and Tricks

Investing in a wood pellet smoker grill is a wonderful idea but it is a significant investment, so you need to make the most of it. To do this, start using the different tips and suggestions discussed in this section. Apart from this, another obvious tip you need to remember while using this appliance is to keep it clean. The buildup of food waste and grime reduces the grill's ability to smoke and cook food properly. By using the different tips discussed in the section, you can up your grilling game within no time. Don't stifle your creativity, experiment with the different recipes given in this book, and cook delicious food!

Understand the Ingredients

Before you start cooking, it is important to understand what you want to cook. Every type of meat needs to be treated differently and every cut differs. By understanding the composition of the meat—whether it has a bone, it's fat content, muscle, and cartilage—you can cook it to perfection. Apart from this, you need to consider the texture of the cut and whether it is dark or white meat. Maybe you want to smoke vegetables or even cheese. Before you start smoking any ingredient in the wood pellet smoker grill, think about what you want to do with it. The great news is, all the recipes you need to make the most of your wood pellet smoker grill are included in this book.

Food Thermometer Helps

Use a thermometer to check the internal temperature of the meat to ensure it cooks better. At times, depending on the cut or fat content of the meat, the cooking time differs. If you don't want to severely over or undercook the meat, using a thermometer will save your time and energy. Investing in a good digital food thermometer will improve the results you obtain by using this grill.

Make the Most of the Upper Racks

Do not forget to utilize the upper racks inside the grill. When you place the meat on them, they are not exposed to direct heat. Instead, they are cooked in a convection mode which yields even results.

By making the most of all the space available in the grill, you can increase the quantity of food that's cooked while making the most of the wood pellets used.

Use a Pizza Attachment

Getting a pizza attachment or stone for the pellet smoker is a wonderful idea. The dome of the smoker grill offers ideal radiant heat to cook pizzas to perfection.

Conclusion

Thank you one again for choosing this book. I hope you enjoyed the recipes and are raring to start your grill.

This book has many easy and delicious wood pellet smoker grill recipes. These recipes are divided into different categories for your convenience. Whether you wish to grill or smoke beef, seafood, poultry, or any other meats including appetizers, sides, and even desserts, there's plenty to choose from. Apart from all this, it also includes several recipes to make delicious homemade marinades, sauces, rubs, and glazes. All these recipes are incredibly simple to understand and easy to cook. As long as you gather the required ingredients and follow the recipe, you can grill or smoke meats and other ingredients to perfection!

While using the wood pellet smoker grill, don't forget to use the various tips and tricks to enhance the cooking results. All the information you need to make the most of your wood pellet smoker grill is provided within this book. Now, all that's left for you to do is select a recipe that you want to cook, gather the necessary ingredients, and get cooking.

Thank you and all the best!

References

Braby, E. (2020, May 10). 9 Pellet Grill Tips and Tricks: Get The Most Out of Your Smoker. Food Fire Friends website: https://www.foodfirefriends.com/pellet-grill-tips/

How Do Pellet Grills Work? Pellet Grills 101 | Pit Boss Grills. (n.d.). pitboss-grills.com website: Https://pitboss-grills.com/pellet-grills-101-how-they-work

Why Should I Try a Pellet Grill, What is it? (2016, August 5). Grilla Grills website: Https://grillagrills.com/why-should-i-try/#:~:text=Pellet%20Grills%20Offer%20a%20Quick%20Heat%20Up&text=Pellet%20grills%20allow%20busy%20people,flavor%20of%20cooking%20over%20wood.

BOOK 3

My Delicious Recipes

Blank Recipe Book to Write In

Adam Greenwood

Common Measurements and Conversions

1 GALLON:
4 quarts
8 pints
16 cups
128 ounces
3.8 liters

1 QUART:
2 pints
4 cups
32 ounces
.95 liters

1 PINT:
2 cups
15 ounces
480 ml

1 CUP:
8 ounces
240 ml

1/4 CUP:
4 Tbsp.
12 tsp.
2 ounces
60 ml

1 Tbsp:
3 tsp.
1/2 ounce
15 ml.

INDEX

RECIPE NAME

	CATEGORY	PAGE
		231
		232
		233
		234
		235
		236
		237
		238
		239
		240
		241
		242
		243
		244
		245
		246
		247
		248
		249
		250

RECIPE NAME

CATEGORY   PAGE

251

252

253

254

255

256

257

258

259

260

261

262

263

264

265

266

267

268

269

270

RECIPE NAME

	CATEGORY	PAGE
		271
		272
		273
		274
		275
		276
		277
		278
		279
		280
		281
		282
		283
		284
		285
		286
		287
		288
		289
		290

RECIPE NAME _____

🕐 PREP TIME
_____

🕐 GRILL TIME
_____

🕐 SMOKE TIME
_____

SERVINGS

INGREDIENTS

_____   _____

_____   _____

_____   _____

_____   _____

_____   _____

_____

DIFFICULTY
○ ○ ○ ○ ○

RATING
○ ○ ○ ○ ○

DIRECTIONS

_____

_____

_____

_____

_____

_____

_____

_____

_____

_____

_____

_____

_____

┌─ NOTES ─────────────────────────────┐
│   │
│   │
│   │
│   │
└──────────────────────────────────────┘

RECIPE NAME _____

⏱ PREP TIME _____ ⏱ GRILL TIME _____ ⏱ SMOKE TIME _____

SERVINGS

INGREDIENTS

_____ _____

_____ _____

_____ _____

_____ _____

_____ _____

DIFFICULTY

○ ○ ○ ○ ○

RATING

○ ○ ○ ○ ○

DIRECTIONS

_____

_____

_____

_____

_____

_____

_____

_____

_____

_____

_____

NOTES

RECIPE NAME _____

⏱ PREP TIME   ⏱ GRILL TIME   ⏱ SMOKE TIME   👥 SERVINGS
_____   _____   _____   ....

INGREDIENTS

_____   _____
_____   _____
_____   _____
_____   _____
_____   _____   DIFFICULTY
_____   _____   ○ ○ ○ ○ ○

                                                 ☆ RATING
                        _____   ○ ○ ○ ○ ○

DIRECTIONS

_____
_____
_____
_____
_____
_____
_____
_____
_____
_____

┌─ NOTES ──────────────────────────────────────┐
│   │
│   │
│   │
│   │
└───┘

RECIPE NAME _____

⏱ PREP TIME _____   🔥 GRILL TIME _____   🔥 SMOKE TIME _____

👥 SERVINGS
....

INGREDIENTS

_____   _____
_____   _____
_____   _____
_____   _____
_____   _____

👨‍🍳 DIFFICULTY
○ ○ ○ ○ ○

⭐ RATING
○ ○ ○ ○ ○

DIRECTIONS

_____
_____
_____
_____
_____
_____
_____
_____
_____
_____

┌─ NOTES ────────────────────────────────────┐
│   │
│   │
│   │
└───┘

RECIPE NAME

PREP TIME

GRILL TIME

SMOKE TIME

SERVINGS

INGREDIENTS

DIFFICULTY

○ ○ ○ ○ ○

RATING

○ ○ ○ ○ ○

DIRECTIONS

NOTES

RECIPE NAME _____

🕐 PREP TIME   🕐 GRILL TIME   🕐 SMOKE TIME

_____   _____   _____

SERVINGS

DIFFICULTY

○ ○ ○ ○ ○

RATING

○ ○ ○ ○ ○

INGREDIENTS

_____   _____

_____   _____

_____   _____

_____   _____

_____   _____

DIRECTIONS

_____

_____

_____

_____

_____

_____

_____

_____

_____

_____

_____

_____

NOTES

RECIPE NAME

PREP TIME _____

GRILL TIME _____

SMOKE TIME _____

SERVINGS

INGREDIENTS

_____   _____

_____   _____

_____   _____

_____   _____

_____   _____

_____   _____

DIFFICULTY

○ ○ ○ ○ ○

RATING

○ ○ ○ ○ ○

DIRECTIONS

_____

_____

_____

_____

_____

_____

_____

_____

_____

_____

_____

_____

_____

_____

NOTES

RECIPE NAME _____

⏱ PREP TIME _____   🍳 GRILL TIME _____   🍳 SMOKE TIME _____

👥 SERVINGS

....

INGREDIENTS

_____   _____

_____   _____

_____   _____

_____   _____

_____   _____

DIFFICULTY

○ ○ ○ ○ ○

☆ RATING

○ ○ ○ ○ ○

DIRECTIONS

_____

_____

_____

_____

_____

_____

_____

_____

_____

_____

_____

_____

_____

┌─ NOTES ──┐
│   │
│   │
│   │
│   │
└───┘

RECIPE NAME _____

PREP TIME
_____

GRILL TIME
_____

SMOKE TIME
_____

SERVINGS
....

INGREDIENTS

_____   _____

_____   _____

_____   _____

_____   _____

_____   _____

DIFFICULTY

○ ○ ○ ○ ○

RATING

○ ○ ○ ○ ○

DIRECTIONS

_____

_____

_____

_____

_____

_____

_____

_____

_____

_____

_____

_____

_____

NOTES

RECIPE NAME _____

⏱ PREP TIME   ⏱ GRILL TIME   ⏱ SMOKE TIME   ┌─────────┐
_____   _____   _____   │   👥   │
                                                             │ SERVINGS │
                                                             │   │
                                                             │ .... │
                                                             └─────────┘

INGREDIENTS

_____   _____
_____   _____   DIFFICULTY
_____   _____   ○ ○ ○ ○ ○
_____   _____
_____   _____   ☆
_____   _____   RATING
                                                            ○ ○ ○ ○ ○

DIRECTIONS

_____
_____
_____
_____
_____
_____
_____
_____
_____
_____
_____
_____

┌─ NOTES ─────────────────────────────┐
│   │
│   │
│   │
│   │
└──────────────────────────────────────┘

RECIPE NAME _____

⏱ PREP TIME   ⏱ GRILL TIME   ⏱ SMOKE TIME   SERVINGS
_____   _____   _____

....

INGREDIENTS

_____   _____
_____   _____
_____   _____   DIFFICULTY
_____   _____   ○ ○ ○ ○ ○
_____   _____
_____   _____   ☆
                                                   RATING
                                                   ○ ○ ○ ○ ○

DIRECTIONS

_____
_____
_____
_____
_____
_____
_____
_____
_____
_____
_____
_____
_____

┌─ NOTES ─────────────────────────────────────┐
│   │
│   │
│   │
│   │
└──┘

RECIPE NAME _____

⏱ PREP TIME _____   ⏱ GRILL TIME _____   ⏱ SMOKE TIME _____

SERVINGS

....

INGREDIENTS

_____   _____
_____   _____
_____   _____
_____   _____
_____   _____

DIFFICULTY

○ ○ ○ ○ ○

RATING

○ ○ ○ ○ ○

DIRECTIONS

_____
_____
_____
_____
_____
_____
_____
_____
_____
_____
_____
_____

NOTES

RECIPE NAME _____

⏱ PREP TIME
_____

⏱ GRILL TIME
_____

⏱ SMOKE TIME
_____

SERVINGS
....

INGREDIENTS

_____   _____
_____   _____
_____   _____
_____   _____
_____   _____
_____   _____

DIFFICULTY
○ ○ ○ ○ ○

☆ RATING
○ ○ ○ ○ ○

DIRECTIONS

_____

_____
_____
_____
_____
_____
_____
_____
_____
_____
_____
_____
_____

NOTES

RECIPE NAME _____

⏱ PREP TIME   ⏱ GRILL TIME   ⏱ SMOKE TIME   👥 SERVINGS
_____   _____   _____   ···········

INGREDIENTS

_____   _____

_____   _____   🎩 DIFFICULTY
                                                                 ○ ○ ○ ○ ○
_____   _____

_____   _____   ⭐ RATING
                                                                 ○ ○ ○ ○ ○
_____   _____

DIRECTIONS

_____

_____

_____

_____

_____

_____

_____

_____

_____

_____

_____

NOTES _____

RECIPE NAME _____

⏱ PREP TIME   ⏱ GRILL TIME   ⏱ SMOKE TIME   SERVINGS
_____   _____   _____

INGREDIENTS

_____   _____

_____   _____   DIFFICULTY
                                                                   ○ ○ ○ ○ ○
_____   _____

_____   _____   RATING
                                                                   ○ ○ ○ ○ ○
_____   _____

DIRECTIONS

_____

_____

_____

_____

_____

_____

_____

_____

_____

_____

_____

_____

┌─ NOTES ───┐
│   │
│   │
│   │
│   │
└──┘

RECIPE NAME _____

⏱ PREP TIME
_____

⏱ GRILL TIME
_____

⏱ SMOKE TIME
_____

👥 SERVINGS
- - - - - - - - - - - -

INGREDIENTS

_____   _____
_____   _____
_____   _____
_____   _____
_____   _____

DIFFICULTY
○ ○ ○ ○ ○

RATING
○ ○ ○ ○ ○

DIRECTIONS

_____
_____
_____
_____
_____
_____
_____
_____
_____
_____
_____

NOTES

RECIPE NAME

PREP TIME _____

GRILL TIME _____

SMOKE TIME _____

SERVINGS
....

INGREDIENTS

_____
_____
_____
_____
_____

_____
_____
_____
_____
_____

DIFFICULTY
○ ○ ○ ○ ○

RATING
○ ○ ○ ○ ○

DIRECTIONS

_____
_____
_____
_____
_____
_____
_____
_____
_____
_____
_____

NOTES

RECIPE NAME _____

⏱ PREP TIME   ⏱ GRILL TIME   ⏱ SMOKE TIME

_____   _____   _____

SERVINGS

INGREDIENTS

_____   _____

_____   _____

_____   _____

_____   _____

_____   _____

DIFFICULTY

○ ○ ○ ○ ○

RATING

○ ○ ○ ○ ○

DIRECTIONS

_____

_____

_____

_____

_____

_____

_____

_____

_____

_____

_____

┌─ NOTES ─────────────────────────────────────┐
│   │
│   │
│   │
│   │
└──┘

RECIPE NAME _____

⏱ PREP TIME   ⏱ GRILL TIME   ⏱ SMOKE TIME   👥
_____   _____   _____   SERVINGS

INGREDIENTS

_____   _____
_____   _____   🎩
_____   _____   DIFFICULTY
_____   _____   ○ ○ ○ ○ ○
_____   _____
                                                                  ☆
                                                                  RATING
                                                                  ○ ○ ○ ○ ○

DIRECTIONS
                                _____

_____
_____
_____
_____
_____
_____
_____
_____
_____
_____
_____
_____

┌─ NOTES ──┐
│   │
│   │
│   │
│   │
└──┘

RECIPE NAME _____

⏱ PREP TIME _____   ⏱ GRILL TIME _____   ⏱ SMOKE TIME _____   SERVINGS

INGREDIENTS

_____   _____
_____   _____
_____   _____
_____   _____
_____   _____

DIFFICULTY
○ ○ ○ ○ ○

RATING
○ ○ ○ ○ ○

DIRECTIONS

_____
_____
_____
_____
_____
_____
_____
_____
_____
_____

NOTES

RECIPE NAME _____

PREP TIME _____   GRILL TIME _____   SMOKE TIME _____

SERVINGS
....

INGREDIENTS

_____   _____
_____   _____
_____   _____
_____   _____
_____   _____

DIFFICULTY
○ ○ ○ ○ ○

RATING
○ ○ ○ ○ ○

DIRECTIONS

_____

_____
_____
_____
_____
_____
_____
_____
_____
_____
_____
_____

NOTES ———————————————————————————————

RECIPE NAME _____

PREP TIME _____

GRILL TIME _____

SMOKE TIME _____

SERVINGS

INGREDIENTS

_____   _____

_____   _____

_____   _____

_____   _____

_____   _____

DIFFICULTY

○ ○ ○ ○ ○

RATING

○ ○ ○ ○ ○

DIRECTIONS

_____

_____

_____

_____

_____

_____

_____

_____

_____

_____

_____

_____

_____

NOTES

RECIPE NAME _____

🕐 PREP TIME   🕐 GRILL TIME   🕐 SMOKE TIME   SERVINGS
_____   _____   _____   ------------------

INGREDIENTS

_____   _____
_____   _____
_____   _____   DIFFICULTY
_____   _____   ○ ○ ○ ○ ○
_____   _____
_____   _____   RATING
_____   _____   ○ ○ ○ ○ ○

DIRECTIONS

_____   _____
_____
_____
_____
_____
_____
_____
_____
_____
_____
_____
_____
_____

NOTES

RECIPE NAME _____

⏱ PREP TIME _____ ⏱ GRILL TIME _____ ⏱ SMOKE TIME _____ 👥 SERVINGS ----------

INGREDIENTS

_____ _____

_____ _____

_____ _____

_____ _____

_____ _____

DIFFICULTY
○ ○ ○ ○ ○

RATING
○ ○ ○ ○ ○

DIRECTIONS

_____

_____

_____

_____

_____

_____

_____

_____

_____

_____

_____

_____

NOTES

RECIPE NAME _____

🕐 PREP TIME   🕐 GRILL TIME   🕐 SMOKE TIME   SERVINGS
_____   _____   _____   ···········

INGREDIENTS

_____   _____
_____   _____
_____   _____   DIFFICULTY
_____   _____   ○ ○ ○ ○ ○
_____   _____
_____   _____   ⭐ RATING
                                                   ○ ○ ○ ○ ○

DIRECTIONS

_____
_____
_____
_____
_____
_____
_____
_____
_____
_____
_____
_____

┌─ NOTES ──────────────────────────────────────
│
│
│
└──

RECIPE NAME _____

⏱ PREP TIME
_____

⏱ GRILL TIME
_____

⏱ SMOKE TIME
_____

SERVINGS
_____

INGREDIENTS

_____ _____

_____ _____

_____ _____

_____ _____

_____

DIFFICULTY
○ ○ ○ ○ ○

RATING
○ ○ ○ ○ ○

DIRECTIONS

_____

_____

_____

_____

_____

_____

_____

_____

_____

_____

_____

_____

NOTES

RECIPE NAME _____

⏱ PREP TIME   ⏱ GRILL TIME   ⏱ SMOKE TIME   👥 SERVINGS
_____   _____   _____   ....

INGREDIENTS

_____   _____

_____   _____

_____   _____

_____   _____

_____   _____

_____   _____

DIFFICULTY

○ ○ ○ ○ ○

RATING

○ ○ ○ ○ ○

DIRECTIONS

_____

_____

_____

_____

_____

_____

_____

_____

_____

_____

_____

NOTES

RECIPE NAME _____

⏱ PREP TIME   ⏱ GRILL TIME   ⏱ SMOKE TIME   👥 SERVINGS
_____   _____   _____   -------------

INGREDIENTS

_____   _____
_____   _____   👨‍🍳 DIFFICULTY
_____   _____   ○ ○ ○ ○ ○
_____   _____
_____   _____   ⭐ RATING
                                                    ○ ○ ○ ○ ○

DIRECTIONS

_____
_____
_____
_____
_____
_____
_____
_____
_____
_____
_____

┌─ NOTES ─────────────────────────────────────┐
│   │
│   │
│   │
└──┘

RECIPE NAME _____

PREP TIME
_____

GRILL TIME
_____

SMOKE TIME
_____

SERVINGS
....

INGREDIENTS

_____ _____
_____ _____
_____ _____
_____ _____
_____ _____
_____ _____

DIFFICULTY
○ ○ ○ ○ ○

RATING
○ ○ ○ ○ ○

DIRECTIONS

_____
_____
_____
_____
_____
_____
_____
_____
_____
_____
_____
_____
_____

┌─ **NOTES** ─────────────────────┐
│   │
│   │
│   │
│   │
└──────────────────────────────────┘

RECIPE NAME _____

🕐 PREP TIME _____   🕐 GRILL TIME _____   🕐 SMOKE TIME _____

SERVINGS
....

INGREDIENTS

_____ _____
_____ _____
_____ _____
_____ _____
_____ _____

DIFFICULTY
○ ○ ○ ○ ○

RATING
○ ○ ○ ○ ○

DIRECTIONS

_____
_____
_____
_____
_____
_____
_____
_____
_____
_____
_____
_____
_____

NOTES

RECIPE NAME _____

🕐 PREP TIME _____   🕐 GRILL TIME _____   🕐 SMOKE TIME _____

SERVINGS

INGREDIENTS

_____   _____
_____   _____
_____   _____
_____   _____
_____   _____
_____   _____

DIFFICULTY

○ ○ ○ ○ ○

☆

RATING

○ ○ ○ ○ ○

DIRECTIONS

_____
_____
_____
_____
_____
_____
_____
_____
_____
_____
_____
_____
_____

┌─ NOTES ────────────────────────────┐
│   │
│   │
│   │
│   │
└─────────────────────────────────────┘

RECIPE NAME _____

⏱ PREP TIME _____ 🔥 GRILL TIME _____ 🔥 SMOKE TIME _____

👥
SERVINGS
....

INGREDIENTS

_____   _____

_____   _____

_____   _____

_____   _____

_____   _____

DIFFICULTY
○ ○ ○ ○ ○

⭐
RATING
○ ○ ○ ○ ○

DIRECTIONS

_____

_____

_____

_____

_____

_____

_____

_____

_____

_____

_____

_____

_____

┌─ NOTES ──────────────────────────────────┐
│   │
│   │
│   │
└───┘

RECIPE NAME _____

⏱ PREP TIME _____   ⏱ GRILL TIME _____   ⏱ SMOKE TIME _____

SERVINGS

....

INGREDIENTS

_____   _____
_____   _____
_____   _____
_____   _____
_____   _____
_____

DIFFICULTY

○ ○ ○ ○ ○

RATING

○ ○ ○ ○ ○

DIRECTIONS

_____
_____
_____
_____
_____
_____
_____
_____
_____
_____
_____
_____

┌─ NOTES ──────────────────────────────────────┐
│   │
│   │
│   │
│   │
└───┘

RECIPE NAME _____

⏱ PREP TIME   ⏱ GRILL TIME   ⏱ SMOKE TIME   👥 SERVINGS

_____   _____   _____   --------------

INGREDIENTS

_____   _____

_____   _____   🎂 DIFFICULTY

_____   _____   ○ ○ ○ ○ ○

_____   _____   ⭐ RATING

_____   _____   ○ ○ ○ ○ ○

DIRECTIONS

_____

_____

_____

_____

_____

_____

_____

_____

_____

_____

_____

_____

┌─ NOTES ──────────────────────────────────┐
│   │
│   │
│   │
│   │
└───┘

RECIPE NAME _____

PREP TIME _____ **GRILL TIME** _____ **SMOKE TIME** _____

SERVINGS

_____

INGREDIENTS

_____ _____

_____ _____

_____ _____

_____ _____

_____ _____

_____ _____

DIFFICULTY

○ ○ ○ ○ ○

RATING

○ ○ ○ ○ ○

DIRECTIONS

_____

_____

_____

_____

_____

_____

_____

_____

_____

_____

_____

_____

NOTES

RECIPE NAME _____

⏱ PREP TIME _____   ⏱ GRILL TIME _____   ⏱ SMOKE TIME _____

SERVINGS

INGREDIENTS

_____   _____
_____   _____
_____   _____
_____   _____
_____   _____

DIFFICULTY
○ ○ ○ ○ ○

RATING
○ ○ ○ ○ ○

DIRECTIONS

_____
_____
_____
_____
_____
_____
_____
_____
_____
_____
_____
_____
_____

┌─ NOTES ──────────────────────────────────────┐
│   │
│   │
│   │
└───┘

RECIPE NAME _____

PREP TIME
_____

GRILL TIME
_____

SMOKE TIME
_____

SERVINGS
....

INGREDIENTS

_____   _____
_____   _____
_____   _____
_____   _____
_____   _____

DIFFICULTY
○ ○ ○ ○ ○

RATING
○ ○ ○ ○ ○

DIRECTIONS

_____
_____
_____
_____
_____
_____
_____
_____
_____
_____
_____
_____

NOTES

RECIPE NAME _____

🕐 PREP TIME   🕐 GRILL TIME   🕐 SMOKE TIME   ┌─────────┐
_____   _____   _____   │   👥   │
                                                                     │ SERVINGS │
                                                                     │   │
                                                                     │ ········· │
                                                                     └─────────┘

INGREDIENTS

_____   _____
_____   _____   DIFFICULTY
_____   _____   ○ ○ ○ ○ ○
_____   _____
_____   _____   ⭐
                                                           RATING
                                                           ○ ○ ○ ○ ○

DIRECTIONS

_____
_____
_____
_____
_____
_____
_____
_____
_____
_____
_____

┌───┐
│ NOTES ─── │
│   │
│   │
│   │
└───┘

RECIPE NAME

PREP TIME

GRILL TIME

SMOKE TIME

SERVINGS

INGREDIENTS

DIFFICULTY

○ ○ ○ ○ ○

RATING

○ ○ ○ ○ ○

DIRECTIONS

NOTES

RECIPE NAME _____

PREP TIME _____ **GRILL TIME** _____ **SMOKE TIME** _____

SERVINGS

INGREDIENTS

_____   _____
_____   _____
_____   _____
_____   _____
_____   _____

DIFFICULTY
○ ○ ○ ○ ○

RATING
○ ○ ○ ○ ○

DIRECTIONS

_____
_____
_____
_____
_____
_____
_____
_____
_____
_____
_____
_____

NOTES

RECIPE NAME _____

PREP TIME _____ GRILL TIME _____ SMOKE TIME _____

SERVINGS

....

INGREDIENTS

_____   _____
_____   _____
_____   _____
_____   _____
_____   _____
_____   _____

DIFFICULTY

○ ○ ○ ○ ○

RATING

○ ○ ○ ○ ○

DIRECTIONS

_____
_____
_____
_____
_____
_____
_____
_____
_____
_____
_____
_____
_____

NOTES

RECIPE NAME _____

🕐 PREP TIME _____   🕐 GRILL TIME _____   🕐 SMOKE TIME _____

SERVINGS

INGREDIENTS

_____   _____

_____   _____

_____   _____

_____   _____

_____   _____

DIFFICULTY

○ ○ ○ ○ ○

RATING

○ ○ ○ ○ ○

DIRECTIONS

_____

_____

_____

_____

_____

_____

_____

_____

_____

_____

_____

NOTES

RECIPE NAME _____

⏱ PREP TIME ⏱ GRILL TIME ⏱ SMOKE TIME 👥 SERVINGS
_____   _____   _____   ....

INGREDIENTS

_____   _____
_____   _____
_____   _____
_____   _____
_____   _____
_____   _____

DIFFICULTY
○ ○ ○ ○ ○

RATING
○ ○ ○ ○ ○

DIRECTIONS

_____
_____
_____
_____
_____
_____
_____
_____
_____
_____
_____
_____

┌─ NOTES ─────────────────────────────────────┐
│   │
│   │
│   │
└──┘

RECIPE NAME _____

⏱ PREP TIME _____   ⏱ GRILL TIME _____   ⏱ SMOKE TIME _____

SERVINGS

INGREDIENTS

_____   _____
_____   _____
_____   _____
_____   _____
_____   _____

DIFFICULTY
○ ○ ○ ○ ○

RATING
○ ○ ○ ○ ○

DIRECTIONS

_____
_____
_____
_____
_____
_____
_____
_____
_____
_____
_____

┌─ NOTES ─────────────────────────┐
│   │
│   │
│   │
└─────────────────────────────────┘

RECIPE NAME

PREP TIME

GRILL TIME

SMOKE TIME

SERVINGS

INGREDIENTS

DIFFICULTY

○ ○ ○ ○ ○

RATING

○ ○ ○ ○ ○

DIRECTIONS

NOTES

RECIPE NAME _____

⏱ PREP TIME   🍖 GRILL TIME   🍖 SMOKE TIME   👥 SERVINGS
_____   _____   _____   ------------

INGREDIENTS

_____   _____
_____   _____   🎂 DIFFICULTY
_____   _____   ○ ○ ○ ○ ○
_____   _____
_____   _____   ⭐ RATING
_____   _____   ○ ○ ○ ○ ○

DIRECTIONS

_____
_____
_____
_____
_____
_____
_____
_____
_____
_____
_____

NOTES

RECIPE NAME _____

⏱ PREP TIME
_____

⏱ GRILL TIME
_____

⏱ SMOKE TIME
_____

SERVINGS
....

INGREDIENTS

_____   _____

_____   _____

_____   _____

_____   _____

_____   _____

_____   _____

DIFFICULTY
○ ○ ○ ○ ○

RATING
○ ○ ○ ○ ○

DIRECTIONS

_____

_____

_____

_____

_____

_____

_____

_____

_____

_____

_____

┌─ NOTES ───┐
│   │
│   │
│   │
│   │
└──┘

RECIPE NAME _____

⏱ PREP TIME
_____

⏱ GRILL TIME
_____

⏱ SMOKE TIME
_____

SERVINGS

INGREDIENTS

_____   _____

_____   _____

_____   _____

_____   _____

_____   _____

DIFFICULTY
○ ○ ○ ○ ○

☆
RATING
○ ○ ○ ○ ○

DIRECTIONS

_____

_____

_____

_____

_____

_____

_____

_____

_____

_____

_____

_____

┌─ NOTES ──────────────────────────────────────┐
│   │
│   │
│   │
│   │
└───┘

RECIPE NAME _____

⏱ PREP TIME   ⏱ GRILL TIME   ⏱ SMOKE TIME

_____   _____   _____

SERVINGS

....

INGREDIENTS

_____   _____

_____   _____

_____   _____

_____   _____

_____   _____

_____   _____

DIFFICULTY

○ ○ ○ ○ ○

RATING

○ ○ ○ ○ ○

DIRECTIONS

_____

_____

_____

_____

_____

_____

_____

_____

_____

_____

_____

_____

NOTES

RECIPE NAME _____

⏱ PREP TIME _____   🔥 GRILL TIME _____   🔥 SMOKE TIME _____

👥 SERVINGS
....

INGREDIENTS

_____   _____

_____   _____

_____   _____

_____   _____

_____   _____

👨‍🍳 DIFFICULTY
○ ○ ○ ○ ○

⭐ RATING
○ ○ ○ ○ ○

DIRECTIONS

_____

_____

_____

_____

_____

_____

_____

_____

_____

_____

_____

┌─ NOTES ─────────────────────────────────────┐
│   │
│   │
│   │
└──┘

RECIPE NAME _____

⏱ PREP TIME   ⏱ GRILL TIME   ⏱ SMOKE TIME   SERVINGS
_____   _____   _____   ----------------

INGREDIENTS

_____   _____
_____   _____
_____   _____   DIFFICULTY
_____   _____   ○ ○ ○ ○ ○
_____   _____
_____   _____   RATING
                                                         ○ ○ ○ ○ ○

DIRECTIONS

_____
_____
_____
_____
_____
_____
_____
_____
_____
_____
_____

NOTES

RECIPE NAME _____

🕐 PREP TIME _____   🕐 GRILL TIME _____   🕐 SMOKE TIME _____

SERVINGS

INGREDIENTS

_____   _____
_____   _____
_____   _____
_____   _____
_____   _____

DIFFICULTY
○ ○ ○ ○ ○

RATING
○ ○ ○ ○ ○

DIRECTIONS

_____
_____
_____
_____
_____
_____
_____
_____
_____
_____
_____
_____

NOTES _____

RECIPE NAME _____

PREP TIME

GRILL TIME

SMOKE TIME

SERVINGS
....

INGREDIENTS

_____   _____
_____   _____
_____   _____
_____   _____
_____   _____

DIFFICULTY

○ ○ ○ ○ ○

RATING

○ ○ ○ ○ ○

DIRECTIONS

_____
_____
_____
_____
_____
_____
_____
_____
_____
_____
_____

NOTES

RECIPE NAME _____

⏱ PREP TIME _____   ⏱ GRILL TIME _____   ⏱ SMOKE TIME _____

SERVINGS

INGREDIENTS

_____   _____
_____   _____
_____   _____
_____   _____
_____   _____
_____   _____

DIFFICULTY
○ ○ ○ ○ ○

RATING
○ ○ ○ ○ ○

DIRECTIONS

_____
_____
_____
_____
_____
_____
_____
_____
_____
_____
_____
_____

NOTES

RECIPE NAME _____

PREP TIME
_____

GRILL TIME
_____

SMOKE TIME
_____

SERVINGS

INGREDIENTS

_____

_____

_____

_____

_____

_____

_____

_____

_____

_____

_____

DIFFICULTY

○ ○ ○ ○ ○

RATING

○ ○ ○ ○ ○

DIRECTIONS

_____

_____

_____

_____

_____

_____

_____

_____

_____

_____

_____

_____

┌─ NOTES ──────────────────────────────┐
│   │
│   │
│   │
│   │
└───────────────────────────────────────┘

RECIPE NAME _____

⏱ PREP TIME _____ 🍖 GRILL TIME _____ 🍖 SMOKE TIME _____

👥 SERVINGS
....

INGREDIENTS

_____   _____

_____   _____

_____   _____

_____   _____

_____   _____

DIFFICULTY
○ ○ ○ ○ ○

⭐ RATING
○ ○ ○ ○ ○

DIRECTIONS

_____

_____

_____

_____

_____

_____

_____

_____

_____

_____

_____

_____

NOTES _____

RECIPE NAME _____

PREP TIME _____ GRILL TIME _____ SMOKE TIME _____

SERVINGS

....

INGREDIENTS

_____   _____

_____   _____

_____   _____

_____   _____

_____   _____

DIFFICULTY

○ ○ ○ ○ ○

RATING

○ ○ ○ ○ ○

DIRECTIONS

_____

_____

_____

_____

_____

_____

_____

_____

_____

_____

_____

_____

NOTES

RECIPE NAME _____

⏱ PREP TIME   🔥 GRILL TIME   🔥 SMOKE TIME   👥 SERVINGS

_____   _____   _____   ---------------

INGREDIENTS

_____   _____

_____   _____

_____   _____

_____   _____

_____   _____

👨‍🍳 DIFFICULTY
○ ○ ○ ○ ○

⭐ RATING
○ ○ ○ ○ ○

DIRECTIONS

_____

_____

_____

_____

_____

_____

_____

_____

_____

_____

_____

NOTES

RECIPE NAME _____

🕐 PREP TIME   🕐 GRILL TIME   🕐 SMOKE TIME   👥 SERVINGS
_____   _____   _____   ----------------

INGREDIENTS

_____   _____

_____   _____   DIFFICULTY
                                                              ○ ○ ○ ○ ○
_____   _____

_____   _____   ☆ RATING

_____   _____   ○ ○ ○ ○ ○

DIRECTIONS

_____

_____

_____

_____

_____

_____

_____

_____

_____

_____

_____

_____

┌─ NOTES ─────────────────────────────────────┐
│   │
│   │
│   │
│   │
└──┘

RECIPE NAME _____

⏱ PREP TIME _____   ⏱ GRILL TIME _____   ⏱ SMOKE TIME _____

SERVINGS

INGREDIENTS

_____   _____

_____   _____

_____   _____

_____   _____

_____   _____

DIFFICULTY
○ ○ ○ ○ ○

RATING
○ ○ ○ ○ ○

DIRECTIONS

_____

_____

_____

_____

_____

_____

_____

_____

_____

_____

_____

_____

NOTES _____

THANK YOU FOR CHOOSING THIS COOKBOOK!

For us, the greatest reward is your satisfaction.

If you liked this item, please support us by leaving a review on Amazon.

Thank you!

Want to write a review now without having to search through your orders?

Turn on your smartphone camera, scan the QR code on the left, and click on the link.

62804238R00162